La Navidad Hispana

at Home and at Church

La Navidad Hispana

at Home and at Church

LITURGY
TRAINING
PUBLICATIONS

Miguel Arias • Mark R. Francis, CSV • Arturo J. Pérez-Rodríguez

Acknowledgments

The English translation of the *posada* song is from Virgilio P. Elizondo and Timothy M. Matovina, *Mestizo Worship, A Pastoral Approach to Liturgical Ministry* (Collegeville, Minnesota: The Liturgical Press, 1998). Used with permission.

Excerpts from the Spanish translation of the *Nicán Mopohua* are reprinted by permission of Obra Nacional de la Buena Prensa, A. C. Excerpts from the English translation of the *Nicán Mopohua* are taken from Virgilio P. Elizondo, *Guadalupe, Mother of the New Creation* (Maryknoll, New York: Orbis Books, 1997). Used with permission.

LA NAVIDAD HISPANA AT HOME AND AT CHURCH © 2000 Archdiocese of Chicago: Liturgy Training Publications, 1800 North Hermitage Avenue, Chicago IL 60622-1101; 1-800-933-1800; fax 1-800-933-7094; orders@ltp.org; www.ltp.org. All rights reserved.

Visit our website at www.ltp.org.

This book was edited by Lorie Simmons. The production editor was Bryan Cones. Larry Cope did the design, and the production artist was Karen Mitchell, who set the book in Minion and Matrix. David A. Lysik translated the rites from Spanish into English. Father Michael Boehm and Father Eduardo Fernández, SJ, provided feedback and additional information. The cover image is by Donna Perrone. Photographs on pages 2, 17 and 50 were taken by Antonio Pérez. Photograph on page 86 was taken by Frances Rivera Alvelo. Printed in Canada by Webcom Limited.

Library of Congress Cataloging-in-Publication Data
Arias, Miguel.
  La Navidad hispana at home and at church / Miguel Arias, Mark R. Francis, Arturo J. Pérez Rodríguez.
    p. cm.
  Includes bibliographical references.
  ISBN 1-56854-357-3 (pbk.)
    1. Advent services — Catholic Church. 2. Christmas service — Catholic Church. 3. Hispanic Americans — Religion. 4. Hispanic American Catholics. 5. Catholic Church — Liturgy — Texts.
  I. Francis, Mark R. II. Perez-Rodriguez, Arturo J. III. Title.
  BX2170.A4 A75 2000
  263.91'089'68073 — dc21   00-057998

LANAV

Dedication

We dedicate this book to Father John Klein (1949–99), who inspired the idea behind this work. Through his entire priestly ministry he served the Hispanic community in Chicago with thoughtfulness and dedication. In his memory we share what the Hispanic community celebrates at Christmastime.

En acción de gracias al Niño Dios, que nos ofreció tan gran regalo en la persona del Padre Juan Klein, quien inspiró la idea y la creación de este libro.

Table of Contents

Foreword

rom the opening lines of *La Navidad Hispana at Home and at Church,* it is clear that liturgical inculturation specialists Arturo Pérez-Rodríguez, Mark Francis and Miguel Arias present us with a delightful and profound yet pastorally practical work that will enrich the liturgical life of our multicultural parishes, whose numbers continue to grow. Typical of these authors' works, *La Navidad Hispana at Home and at Church* reveals their ability to listen to the collective voice of Hispanic people — their cultural heart and common memory — which longs for recognition, acceptance, respect and celebration.

Although it is grounded on solid liturgical principles, this is definitely not a theoretical work. Rather, it is the work of creative ministers who know their people well, have a passion for the Hispanic religious heritage, and are dedicated to the liturgical life of the church. They are not just interested in religious traditions, however, but in the living faith of people. From their own personal experience they know well how the religious expressions of one cultural group can be a source of enrichment to another. Far from being divisive, cultural difference can enrich everyone, bringing about a deeper and more exciting unity. This is truly the work of the Spirit.

One of the great traits of this book, along with its predecessor, *Primero Dios,* is that it does not begin with generalities but with fictional stories based on people and situations from the authors' pastoral experience. From the beginning we are invited to enter the lives of people and their families, witnessing their sense of community and their struggle not only for survival but for a meaningful existence, especially in the realm of religion. The stories show how celebrations from their Hispanic religious heritage connect people to their homelands, which many of them were forced to leave behind. The characters who prepare and celebrate the liturgies in these narratives give to this pastoral guide for liturgical planning the excitement and intrigue of a good novel.

Another great quality of this work is the ability of the authors to weave together into a beautiful quilt the various traditions that express our Catholic faith. The biblical, the Western European and the *mestizo* come together to create something uniquely "American." Just as the church has been nourished by the traditions of Eastern and Western Christianity over the course of history, now a new, distinctly American tradition is emerging, and this simple but exciting book makes a great contribution to that new tradition. By connecting these native religious practices with the other religious traditions of the United States, the authors help people become part of a greater family—a true family of nations.

꙳꙳

La Navidad Hispana at Home and at Church provides the reader with beautiful and practical insights for creating new liturgical expressions in multicultural parishes that truly include everyone. It envisions a parish that doesn't just tolerate differences but indeed celebrates the unique characteristics of each group as enriching for all. This work is an excellent initiation into greater and more exciting things to come.

It is especially meaningful that *La Navidad Hispana at Home and at Church* is dedicated to my good friend, Father John Klein. I first met John when he came to the Mexican American Cultural Center as a young deacon along with his classmates Michael Boehm and Don Nevins. We instantly became friends, and from that moment on, I have marveled at the love and commitment that all three of them have exhibited throughout the years, not just for Latino religious cultures but for all the struggles of the poor to obtain a better life. Though not Latino by birth, they surely became Latino *de corazón*. John Klein has left this present life, but his priestly ministry and dedication continue to enrich the parishes he served and the many people he touched through his work, especially as it is reflected in this beautiful book dedicated to his memory. Truly, he is not dead; he has been transformed.

Virgilio Elizondo
Mexican American Cultural Center
May 10, 2000

El Espíritu Navideño:
The Spirit of Christmas in the
Hispanic Community

isten to this conversation between a new non-Hispanic pastor and his Hispanic pastoral associate in a multicultural urban parish in the United States:

Father, it's already the middle of November, and there are still some details to our Advent and Christmas planning that we need to attend to. Let me just run down the list with you to give you an idea of what we need to think about. The *Guadalupanas* are already busy collecting funds and organizing the novena, but we need to sit down with the musicians and plan the *Mañanitas* celebration for December 12. We also need to think about how we can involve our catechists in helping set up several *posadas* for the different neighborhoods within the parish as we did last year. Also, let's think about suggesting to the various groups that

we spend more time explaining the catechetical origin of the piñatas this year. Both the Puerto Ricans and Filipinos are asking if we would be willing to sponsor a *Misa de aguinaldo* or *Simbang Gabi*. This would be an excellent way of bringing these two groups together with the rest of the parish. We also need to plan with the liturgy committee how we are going to celebrate the *acostamiento del Niño Dios* at the Midnight Mass this year. I also feel strongly that we should encourage the youth group to put on a *pastorela* after Christmas. I have the script ready, and I could help direct the production. And just between us, I think you need to prepare yourself for an *asalto* the day after Christmas. I overheard the Puerto Rican *parranderos* speaking about this as a nice way of helping you celebrate your first year in the parish. There are a few other post-Christmas customs you need to be aware of, but we can speak about those later.

Unsuspecting pastors and other pastoral ministers in Hispanic parishes have often been confronted with the dizzying array of Hispanic Advent and Christmas traditions, often without any idea as to their significance. Unfortunately, in many parishes these traditions are at best tolerated or at worst dismissed as quaint but irrelevant folk customs. Many pastoral leaders, including some Hispanics, are unaware that in addition to affirming cultural identity these customs were originally created by the early missionaries to the Americas as culturally appropriate vehicles of evangelization. Practices as diverse as *posadas* in the Mexican community and *Misas de aguinaldo* among Puerto Ricans helped catechists enact the scriptures for new Christians. For centuries these customs have continued to root the Good News of Jesus Christ in the lives of Latin Americans.

The Deeper Issue: Culture and Worship

As we begin the third millennium of Christianity, the church is becoming more conscious of the way that culture has influenced liturgy over the course of Christian history. In previous ages, many of our ancestors in faith took for granted that our inherited forms of prayer were divinely ordained (and believed economic and political structures were as well). Our worship changed so slowly that the majority of Catholics never realized that many of the liturgical practices they thought were universal were really quite particular, heavily influenced by local traditions, languages and symbols.

Even after the Council of Trent, when rigid liturgical uniformity was emphasized as the supreme value, the Roman rite was experienced in different ways due to its various cultural contexts. The Mass in Italy, Ireland and Austria might have been identical according to the liturgical books, but the arrangement and appointments of the worship space (its art and environment), the music used at the celebration, and the folk customs associated with a particular feast before and after the celebration in church all made the universal rite particular and meaningful to a given people. For example, the custom of the Advent wreath with four candles to mark the four Sundays of Advent comes

from a northern European custom practiced in the home and is not offi-
cially part of the liturgy of the Roman rite.

Around the turn of the twentieth century, "national"
parishes were established in the United States for the many immigrant
groups that were pouring into the country from southern and eastern
Europe. In these parishes the newcomers could celebrate the faith in
familiar ways and could preserve their cultural identity in a secular environment that pressured all groups to assimilate. Even though Mass was
celebrated in Latin, pastoral effectiveness demanded that ministers
preach in the language of the people, use their symbols, and celebrate
their saints. In short, even for the "unchanging" Tridentine liturgy to be
effective, it had to celebrate the mystery of Christ using the cultural
forms of the people at worship.

Today the U.S. Catholic church is experiencing a similar
pastoral and liturgical challenge, occasioned by another wave of immi-
gration. In addition to the growing number of Asians (Filipinos,
Vietnamese and Koreans, to name a few) and Africans (as well as a new
sensitivity to African American cultural differences), the Hispanic presence in the U.S. Catholic church is being felt more and more in parishes
around the country.

The *Mística*

Unlike some cultures that are only recently evangelized or those that are
not traditionally Catholic, the various Hispanic groups coming to this
country have what can be termed a "Catholic culture." It would be a mis-
take, however, to think that all Hispanic groups are the same. Even the
term "Hispanic" is not universally accepted; some prefer the adjective
"Latino" or even "Hispanic-Latino." For the purposes of this book,
"Hispanic" and "Latino" will be used interchangeably.

Despite their differences, peoples as diverse as Mexicans, Cubans and Chileans share a *mística,* or worldview, that is conditioned by centuries of contact with the gospel. The *mística* is the way Latinos conceive of their place in the world and their relationship to God and to other human beings. The term also refers to a spirituality that comes from deeply held values such as the dignity of the individual, the centrality of the family, and the importance given to feeling and sentiment in living an authentically Christian life.

From a historical perspective, the *mística* is the result of a clash of three cultural worlds: European, Native American and African. Through the *mestizaje* (mixing) of the Iberian conquerors with the native peoples of America and slaves from Africa, a new *raza* was born— a people that incorporated aspects of all three cultures. This *mestizaje* is especially evident in the Hispanic approach to liturgy and prayer, and influences the way Latinos interpret the traditional Catholic liturgical year. A casual observer will note, for example, that the rhythm of the liturgical year is a bit different in Hispanic parishes. In fact, one could almost say that there is a "Hispanic" liturgical year that is based on the Roman version but emphasizes the personal and relational over the abstract and doctrinal. For example, the Good Friday practice of reenacting the way of the cross and setting aside time to offer *el pésame a la Virgen* (condolences to Mary as the sorrowful mother) expresses the human, personal relationship with Jesus, Mary and the saints that is the cornerstone of Hispanic popular religion.

The lens through which many Hispanics interpret their Catholic faith is popular religion. Rituals and beliefs handed down in the home express the *mística* and form a large part of popular religion, giving a human face to the more formal catechism of the institutional church. Popular religious practice can include a mother or father blessing their children before they run out the door to play. It can also take the form of a home altar, or *altarcito*, usually tended by the mother of the family, which highlights the sacredness of the home.

Popular religious practices tend to be dramatic and emotional. As mentioned earlier, some of them, such as Christmas and Easter plays, have their origin in the first efforts of the Franciscan, Dominican and Augustinian missionaries to teach the faith to the native peoples through drama. Attending to the people's own religious customs—some of which differ from group to group—is an important aspect of ministry with Hispanics and crucial for inculturating the liturgy. One must also keep in mind that, while these rites are traditionally celebrated in Spanish, there may be a significant number of Hispanics whose primary language is English. Although they feel culturally connected to the rites, these people are better served by bilingual celebrations.

Time and the Hispanic Community

It would not come as a shock to most people with even a limited experience of Latino parishes that many Hispanics have a sense of time that is different from non-Hispanics. While this sense of time often affects when meetings and liturgies begin (late), it is also undeniable that once a celebration is underway, most Latinos are capable of sustaining festivity in a way that ethnic groups more tied to the clock are not. This sense of time and capacity for celebration also affects the way the seasons are observed. In some ways, the Hispanic approach is the more traditional manner that Christians through the centuries have observed the liturgical year. While modern U.S. society seems "Christmased-out" by December 26, a high level of festive energy is apparent among Hispanics all the way to Epiphany (January 6) and, for some, even the feast of the Presentation of the Lord, *Candelaria* (February 2). Whereas non-Hispanic communities need to explain to children how Christmas could have twelve days when they ask about the old English Christmas carol "The twelve days of Christmas," no such explanation would be necessary for Hispanics, since many commonly observe twelve days of celebration. For this reason, in addition to enhancing hospitality to Latinos, a sensitivity to Hispanic customs during this period of the year may help non-Hispanics recapture some of the original dynamism that gave rise to the liturgical year in the first place.

Our Approach to Ministry in Hispanic Communities: Listen to the People

A basic tenet of good pastoral ministry is that ministers should listen to the people with whom they minister and attend to their experience of the faith as it is lived through their popular religiosity. For the purposes of this book, listening—understood in the broad sense—will focus on what Latino parishioners and others have to say about their Christmas celebrations. We are convinced that Hispanic traditions and customs, although perhaps strange and unfamiliar to non-Hispanics, are not only capable of injecting new life and new enthusiasm into parish celebrations but are the basis for culturally appropriate and ongoing evangelization.

In order to situate these traditions in a realistic context, we will present each Hispanic Advent or Christmas custom first in a narrative that portrays specific situations in the religious life of a fictional family in a multicultural urban parish. By doing so, we can come to appreciate how these Hispanic traditions celebrate the relationships of Hispanics to God, to each other, and to the universe. Reflections following each vignette will focus on the pastoral issues raised by the story.

Our descriptions of these customs are not meant to exhaust the richness of the Hispanic approach to Christmas as observed by the various peoples who are now an integral part of the U.S. Catholic church. Rather, the brief reflections on the Hispanic customs of a given season are intended for the pastoral minister who may not be familiar with some of these traditions but who wants to be sensitive to their appropriate incorporation into the liturgical life of the parish.

Finally, these reflections are not limited to the liturgy strictly speaking but address the wide range of customs that give meaning to the various celebrations of the liturgical year. It has been said that successful Hispanic religious celebrations are holistic experiences, appealing to all the senses. They also extend beyond the church and reach into the home.

We will present these celebrations in the context of a multicultural, predominantly Hispanic parish. Much like our first volume on Hispanic culture and liturgy, *Primero Dios,* we hope that this book will enrich the pastoral ministry of those serving Latino communities. It is a small contribution toward helping the church in the United States take seriously the continual need for the inculturation of pastoral ministry, since, as Pope John Paul II has observed, "A faith that does not become culture is a faith not fully accepted, not entirely thought out, not faithfully lived" (letter instituting the Pontifical Council for Culture, May 20, 1982).

The Setting for Our Story: San Martín de Porres Parish

San Martín de Porres Parish has always been in a state of constant change. When it was founded more than one hundred years ago, it was home to eastern European immigrants who needed their own place of worship and was built as a living monument to the way that the Catholic faith was lived at that time. When the first Hispanics moved into the neighborhood, they also felt at home in the building, although tensions and conflicts arose between the groups. Mistakes were made and feelings were hurt, but life continued and the practice of the faith was like an anointing that soothed wearied spirits. The parish church came to reflect the best of both cultural and religious worlds, especially when the entire community, founders and newcomers, agreed to renovate the church's interior space. When finished, it gleamed with the aura of the community that it served. The mystery of God continued to dwell within its walls.

Just as that mystery cannot be captured, so too a parish does not stand still. A new change quietly took place. The hurricanes, natural disasters and political unrest that swept Central America during the 1990s brought waves of new people to the neighborhood. At the same time, the state medical complex was expanded, stretching to within three blocks of the parish church. Medical personnel, many from the Philippines, moved into the neighborhood to live close to their place of work. San Martín also had to stretch, not only to accommodate the newcomers who sought comfort and shelter but to embrace them as well. This new expansion brought changes in the way the parish practiced its religious life.

One of the changes came in the form of small base communities. These base communities gathered neighbors together in each other's homes to discuss scripture, its relevance to their lives, and what action they would take as a result of their prayerful discernment. Through this process, new leadership developed.

Rutilio was a "glassman" by trade, which is what they called him at The Scot's Bar, where he worked. He had gotten the job through his *compadre* Jon, who had heard about it from his wife's cousin. Rutilio had become a legal resident through the amnesty program. He was moving toward middle age, though it was hard to tell from his youthful appearance. His job was to keep the bustling tavern and restaurant supplied with clean glassware, and from the artistic and practical way he arranged the many shapes of glasses, it was evident that Rutilio took pride in his work. He also took pride in bringing his gifts to San Martín, where he was a recognized leader of a small base community.

Rutilio's wife, Silvia, was his equal in every way. Their relationship was so natural that they could almost read each other's thoughts by just looking into the other's eyes. While her husband was an immigrant, Silvia was a migrant farmworker's daughter. Her mother had brought her up almost alone—almost, because Silvia's grandparents, Papá Ramón and Mamá Pachita, had lent a helping hand. It was from them that Silvia learned the old ways of *papel picado,* or piñata-making, along with the songs, foods and stories that accompanied the passing of the seasons. These traditions required no elaborate materials. They fit into a life that was made from leftovers and scraps, but it was life—their life—and always worth celebrating.

Chino was Rutilio and Silvia's third child. Though out of high school, he still lived at home. His mother called him "liquid eyes," for his were deep, black, shining and alive; one was never sure what was going on behind them. As much as he wanted independence, he was still tied to his parents because he found in their base community a family of friends who shared his concerns and doubts about the neighborhood, life, God and his friends.

Chino's sister Lola was christened María Dolores de la Soledad, a name she said was too heavy for her to bear. Her declaration of freedom had come during her *quinceañera* celebration the year before, when she publicly announced that she would no longer respond to the name Dolores but wanted to be known as Lola. Nothing in her behavior changed. She continued to go to school and attend confirmation classes. And she continued to be an independent, strong-willed young woman growing in wisdom and grace, but now as Lola.

Father John, always looking for a new challenge, was transferred from an African American parish and named pastor of San Martín de Porres. While he studied Spanish at a language school in Cochabamba, Bolivia, he also immersed himself in a local Bolivian parish. This experience taught him the value of *Comunidades Eclesiales de Base.* When he returned to the United States, he became one of the main proponents of the base community approach for San Martín. These small communities brought new life to the parish through the ideas that were generated in the home meetings. Was he busier than before? Not really, he thought, just more and more open to his parishioners' lives. He was impressed by their willingness to go the extra mile to get to know one another. This had proven to be especially helpful when new people began to arrive in the parish; misunderstandings were minimal. Father John and the council of base community leaders met regularly to pray, plan and celebrate their parish's life. He relied heavily on Rutilio and Silvia, cochairs of the liturgy committee.

Before Christmas

he night walk home from the parish didn't take very long, ten minutes at the most. An early snow was beginning to cover the cars, sidewalks and streets in a way that made everything glisten in the glow of the streetlights. The snowfall temporarily hid all the broken and cracked pavement. As they walked home, Silvia and Rutilio shared their skepticism about the ideas that the liturgy committee had generated.

The group had discussed how Advent was going to be celebrated this year. It was evident that equal amounts of time for liturgy would be spent in the base communities and in the church. In order for everyone to celebrate well together, it was necessary to develop a more structured format for the small-group Advent services; that format would then be reflected in the major events, when all the groups gathered together at the church. Trying to explain and celebrate the Advent season, enriched as it was in their parish by the many homeland traditions, seemed to be a task worthy of Solomon. Advent, with its winter wreath, four candles and subdued colors, contrasted sharply with the festive celebration of the Guadalupe novena and the observance of the actual feast day itself, with its early morning serenade and red rose splendor. There was also the problem of making a smooth transition to the Mexican *posadas,* the Filipino *posadas* (called the *panuluyan* celebration, which would be celebrated at San Martín for the first time this year), the Puerto Rican *parrandas* and, finally, Christmas Eve Mass.

Rutilio and Silvia felt uncertain not about what was to be done but about how they would manage their community responsibilities and still work, take care of the family, and motivate their neighbors to do the same. Rutilio recalled Silvia's important contribution to the meeting when she related something that her grandparents had taught her. Since her family was on the road so much, they always had to improvise, responding to changing situations. The same wisdom could serve the people of San Martín. Advent and Christmas traditions did not have to be celebrated exactly the same way every year. Silvia helped the group see that each Advent was basically a preparation for Christ to enter their lives in a new way.

The liturgy committee believed that each of the pre-Christmas traditions of their various cultures was a living word in the Advent gospel preached in their parish. It was decided that the base communities would follow a common format for prayer but be free to adapt it as they thought best. Inclusivity, as usual, would be the core value, so that those who gathered would feel they had contributed and shared a part of their Christmas history and tradition. The task was formidable but not impossible.

"Primero Dios," Silvia said, as she and Rutilio climbed the stairs and opened the front door of their home, leaving the snow to cover their tracks.

The Guadalupe Novena

The novena had gone better than planned. Each of the base communities was assigned a night to lead the Guadalupe novena for all those who wanted to be in the church during these days. Meanwhile, the other communities continued to meet in different homes to pray the rosary and the novena prayers, read the gospel from the Mass of the day, offer intercessory prayer, sing a Marian hymn, and share something warm to drink before returning home. Every night a particular tradition of the season was highlighted by one of the families at the base community gatherings. The members of the communities learned about the meaning of these days in their different cultures. But the feast of Guadalupe was one of the events that everyone celebrated in the church as a parish family.

December 12, the feast of Our Lady of Guadalupe, found Father John opening the front doors of the church at 4:00 AM. More than twenty people anxious to get in greeted him. Chino and Lola, still sleepy, had been sent on ahead of their parents to pass out candles and help make the final arrangements.

The service began in semidarkness around 5:00 AM. Father John, led by one of the base community leaders carrying the paschal candle, greeted the people at the front door of the church. The assembly offered a prayer of greeting to Mary as the Morning Star, which had become a parish tradition, and as the people reached out to light their candles from the paschal candle, they sang "Las mañanitas."

The flames from the candles glowed warmly as the procession entered. The Guadalupe image, ornamented with colorful women's *rebozos* (shawls) was surrounded by the four tall Advent candles. This year, men's hats, characteristic of the various cultural groups, accompanied the shawls. Rutilio's job was to light a taper from the paschal candle and then light the first two Advent candles as Chino turned on the church lights. The Virgin of Guadalupe became an Advent icon, a presence in dialogue with the people of San Martín.

The *Posadas* Novena

When Father John first arrived at the parish an elderly couple presented him with a large wooden box. They were childless, the last living members of their respective families in the United States, and they wanted to make a donation to the parish. They carefully unwrapped the contents of the box, revealing a three-foot statue of Mary seated on a donkey being led by Joseph. The statue of the holy *peregrinos* (pilgrims) had belonged to the elderly man's parents. Amazed at the workmanship and detail, Father John repeated his gratitude as the couple walked out the door. He stood absorbed in thought as he watched them disappear down the street.

December 16 marked the first night of the *posadas*. The Guadalupe image resumed its usual place of honor in the church and was replaced by the century-old *posada* statue. The base communities had celebrated the beginning of this Advent novena by walking the cold streets of their neighborhoods. Chino and Lola, elected youth leaders from their base community, would lead tonight's parish *posada*. These parish gatherings stressed youth involvement and initiative. The format for prayer was the same as that used in the neighborhoods.

Arriving early, Chino and Lola carefully brought the *posada* statue to the entrance of the church, carrying it as if the figures were family friends they hadn't seen for a long time. Both felt a vivid sense of the Holy Family's presence through the statue, a presence in which they would have liked to linger. But the sound of laughter signaled the arrival of the young people and reminded them of their obligations.

When all was ready, Lola stood with the families at the front inner doors while Chino accompanied another group through the doors and into the church. San Martín had been built with an indoor gathering space in front of an interior set of doors, and now this space protected everyone from the winter cold. As was customary, the traditional sung dialogue between the two groups repeated the pilgrim's story: strangers looking for shelter. The story taught the young people that life's beginning is not easy, even for the Savior. With each sung stanza the group moved slowly into the church and more deeply into the story of new life. Chino and Lola led the rosary and novena prayers. They also led the celebration in the church hall, where a piñata was broken and refreshments served. Before closing the church, Chino and Lola said their goodbyes to the *posada* figures and prayed for the elderly couple who had brought them such a wonderful gift.

Pastoral Notes

Advent and Guadalupe: Complementary Rather Than Conflictive

Advent in the Hispanic community may at first appear to be problematic, yet it holds a great pastoral opportunity. Liturgical and cultural symbols that seem to clash actually overlap, complement and enhance one another.

While we need not explain here the meaning of Advent or retell in detail the history of the Guadalupe apparitions (the bibliography recommends resources on these subjects), we do want to highlight the themes each expresses. Advent is usually presented as a solemn time that calls for reflection on both the second coming of Christ at the end of the world and his first coming in the incarnation. The prophets Isaiah, Jeremiah, Zephaniah and John the Baptist foretell what Mary's pregnancy makes real for us: the promise of a new age, a new beginning about to be born. This metaphor of pregnancy gives us the main theme of the season: preparation. At this time we reflect on God's promise fulfilled once in the past to Israel and our hope and preparation for its final fulfillment for all people in the future.

The northern European Advent wreath with its four candles has become a distinctive liturgical symbol that marks the passing of the Advent weeks. Although the church's diversity embraces rites that still maintain six weeks of preparation for Christmas, along with traditions in the Eastern churches that include Marian observances as stepping-stones to Christmas, four weeks of Advent are standard for most Catholic Christians in the United States. The tradition of lighting one candle in the wreath each week along with the purple vestments of the presider convey a quiet, meditative tone.

CHAPTER 2

~~~~~

In the midst of this quiet solemnity appears Our Lady of Guadalupe, patroness of Mexico, empress of all the Americas. (This celebration is now a feast in the liturgical calendars of North and South America.) She appears to a conquered people who are suffering cultural annihilation, and she incarnates the promise of God that gives them hope as they become a new people, a *mestizo* race. Juan Diego and his uncle, Juan Bernardino, take on prophetic roles as they announce to the authorities of the day her message: A church is to be built at the Mount of Tepeyac, the sanctuary of Tonantzin, the Aztec mother goddess. The new place of worship, outside the geography of power and authority of that time, sheds gospel light on the old Aztec beliefs, bringing forth a new expression of faith. Guadalupe is one with those who suffer; she identifies with their sacred places and traditions.

The narrative of the apparitions, the novena prayers and the feast day help the people prepare for the fulfillment of God's promise then and now. Guadalupe is the Virgin Mary, but from an indigenous perspective; she manifests the feminine image and expression of God that bears the Son of promise to all people. Hispanic theologians such as Virgilio Elizondo have proposed that no other event since Pentecost has had such a profound impact as Our Lady of Guadalupe. She reveals God's hope for humanity. This is Advent in a Hispanic context; this is the Advent gospel culturally proclaimed.

Posadas and Other Events

The pre-Christmas events described here combine two traditions that may be unfamiliar to contemporary North Americans. The style of prayers is mantra-like, meant to give an external order to an interior reality. They repeat over and over the same phrase, such as "Prepare the way of the Lord."

Posadas are an example of Hispanic prayer dramatically enacted. They are celebrated in various ways in countries like Mexico, Belize, Guatemala, Panama and Nicaragua; in the Philippines they are known as *panuluyan. Posadas* usually take place during the nine evenings before Christmas. A dialogue sung between two groups takes place at a doorway—the symbolic bridge between two realities. The prayers of the people are intercessory, expressing solidarity with a man and a woman, pilgrims seeking shelter from strangers, as well as comfort and compassion from their neighbors. This drama forms part of the Advent novena. It highlights the mystery of God's presence in ordinary human interactions, reminding us that the One who was not recognized by his neighbors has become the cornerstone for a new community of believers.

Other types of novena Masses may mark the days before Christmas. Filipinos celebrate *Simbang Gabi,* while Puerto Ricans and other Latino groups celebrate *Misas de aguinaldo.*

Traditionally, all of these rites include the recitation of the rosary. In Hispanic tradition the rosary often begins with a prayer for forgiveness, sometimes using the Confiteor from the penitential rite of Mass.

The novenas for the feast of Guadalupe and the *posadas* usually end with piñatas and refreshments. The Franciscan missionaries originally used piñatas as catechetical tools, teaching that their customary seven projections represented the seven capital sins. The game of hitting the piñatas with sticks represented the faithful person's continuous struggle with Satan in order to regain the grace that Satan had taken away. When the piñata was broken, "grace"—candy, fruit and favors— poured down.

The Puerto Rican *parrandas,* also called *pollos* in the Dominican Republic, usually take place after Christmas but sometimes occur before. These are nocturnal *asaltos,* or raids, made upon friends and relatives at their homes. The noisy revelers, who are often talented amateur musicians, sing and play their guitars at the front door to wake the householders from their sleep, "demanding" to be shown hospitality even at a most inconvenient hour. The *parranda* "demand" to be fed parallels the gospel image of a man asking to borrow food from his sleeping neighbor.

Justice themes appear throughout these pre-Christmas events. As Mary and Joseph in the *posadas* seek welcome but are often rejected, newcomers are often turned away in our society. The Christmas traditions of *Junkanoo* or *Los Guloyas*, which developed among slaves and are found in different forms in Belize and the Dominican Republic, express the identity of another group of people denied justice. Believed to have begun in the sixteenth and seventeenth centuries, when slaves were allowed to perform their African music and dance only at Christmas, these practices became a celebration of their past, their freedom and their traditions of faith.

Advent *Ambiente*

The Advent ambience of the church is a constant reminder that we as a Christian people are continually in preparation, continually changing and moving. Imbued with the faith experience of the people, the Hispanic feast days of this season tangibly enact that Christian journey. Each celebration is a step in the journey; each tells a story of preparation. The Guadalupe feast is followed by the *posadas*, then *Nochebuena* (Christmas Eve).

This active Advent cycle defines time as *kairos* rather than *chronos*, sacred time rather than secular. In other words, these celebrations are an encounter with the sacred and not just the reasons to turn pages on the calendar. They are the ways that Hispanics touch the mystery of God's unfolding presence. Though not all Hispanic communities place the same emphasis on each event or relate the same meaning to every feast, the common theme—we are preparing for or celebrating Christmas—is present. This places a challenging demand upon the pastoral minister, a demand made even more confusing by liturgical preparation guides for Advent, which usually prescribe a reflective tone for Advent celebrations.

Reflection takes place in different ways in different cultures. The act of preparing or waiting for something is not always a quiet affair. Anticipation can sometimes be noisy and gleeful. A sparse, quiet, meditative atmosphere does not necessarily fit Hispanic sensibilities. Hispanics are a young people; children make up at least one third of the community, with youth and young parents making up the majority. In this context, movement and commotion will be constant. Indeed, in the southwestern United States, Native American dancers called *matachines* play a key role in these celebrations and perform *danza* (sacred dance) as a form of prayer. Novena prayers, flowers, guitar music, colorful displays and traditional hymns ritualize that movement and proclaim the season's message: "Get ready for the Son of promise to be born."

Advent and Guadalupe symbols must be creatively interwoven. Reflection is not static but is a dynamic process that sees the gospel message in the events being celebrated. The liturgical and cultural symbols of these days mutually enhance one another.

Nuestra Señora de Guadalupe, celebración en el templo

Este modelo se propone para que en las comunidades que no cuentan con un sacerdote para presidir la celebración, sea un diácono, catequista o un miembro de la comunidad quien presida la celebración. Ayudará mucho el proveer las indicaciones necesarias para la asamblea y la letra de los cantos, para así lograr una mayor participación del pueblo. Se debe notificar a la asamblea que es necesario que traigan velas para esta celebración, al menos que la parroquia quiera proveerlas.

La gente se ha reunido ya. Los ministros y algunos representantes de la comunidad se reunen a la entrada del templo, alrededor de la pila bautismal (si ésta se encuentra a la entrada) y con una oscuridad casi total que se irá iluminando de forma gradual. El diácono u otro ministro llevará el cirio pascual previamente encendido, del cual se encenderán las velas que han traído o recibido de los ujieres.

I. RITOS INICIALES

Saludo
El que preside, santiguándose la frente con agua bendita, pronunciará el saludo inicial y continuará el esquema de la celebración.

El que preside: Señor, abre mis labios:
R: Y mi boca proclamará tu alabanza.

El que preside: Gloria al Padre, al Hijo y al Espíritu Santo:
R: Como era en el principio, ahora y siempre, por los siglos de los siglos. Amén.

El que preside: Mi corazón en amarte, eternamente se ocupe,
R: Y mi lengua en alabarte, madre mía de Guadalupe.

El que preside: Queridos hermanos y hermanas, nos reunimos al romper el alba para saludar a la Señora del cielo, reconociendo en ella el escudo de nuestra fe; recordamos también

Our Lady of Guadalupe, Celebration in the Church

This rite has been developed so that the presider may be a deacon, catechist or other member of the community. In order to facilitate participation, it is highly recommended that a worship aid containing song lyrics and directions for the assembly be given to all. The people should be notified that they need to bring candles for the celebration unless the parish will provide them.

The people gather in the church, which is almost totally dark. The ministers and some representatives of the community stand at the entrance of the church building (near the baptismal font, if it is located at the entrance). Accompanying the presider is a deacon or other minister carrying the paschal candle, from which the faithful will light the candles they brought with them or received from the ushers.

I. INTRODUCTORY RITES

Greeting

The presider makes the sign of the cross on his or her forehead using holy water and greets those present with the following or similar words.

> *Presider:* Lord, open my lips:
> *R:* And my mouth will proclaim your praise.
>
> *Presider:* Glory to the Father, and to the Son, and to the Holy Spirit:
> *R:* As it was in the beginning, is now and will be for ever. Amen.
>
> *Presider:* May my heart ever love you,
> *R:* And my tongue ever praise you, O Lady of Guadalupe.
>
> *Presider:* My brothers and sisters, we gather at the break of dawn to honor the holy Virgin Mary, whose life is an example for our faith. We also recall God's presence in the history of the peoples

que Dios se hizo presente en la historia de los pueblos latino-
americanos de diferentes maneras, en particular se hizo presente
en México con las apariciones de la Santísima Virgen. Ella hace
de Juan Diego, su embajador ante el obispo, dejando claro una
vez más que Dios está del lado del pobre, pero sobre todo de
aquellos que buscan la luz en medio de las tinieblas de su propia
vida. Celebremos nuestra fe en Jesucristo como un solo pueblo,
de toda raza, lengua y nación, y nuestra devoción a su Santísima
Madre, quien aun desea un templo en cada corazón humano y
en cada cultura representada en esta casa del Señor.

Canto inicial: "Buenos días paloma blanca"

*Las velas de la asamblea se irán encendiendo en la medida en que los
ministros se dirigen hacia el presbiterio. Una vez ahí, cada ministro tomará
su lugar correspondiente. El cirio pascual se colocará cerca de la imagen de
la Virgen de Guadalupe.*

Oración colecta

> *El que preside:*
> Oremos.
> Padre de misericordia,
> tú que has concedido a toda América
> la protección especial de la Virgen María,
> nuestra Señora de Guadalupe;
> concédenos permanecer firmes en la fe,
> servir con sincero amor a nuestros hermanos y hermanas
> y buscar el progreso de nuestras naciones
> por caminos de justicia y de paz,
> por nuestro Señor Jesucristo.
> *R:* Amén

*Las velas permanecerán encendidas hasta que inicie la lectura de las
apariciones.*

of Latin America in various ways; in particular we recall God's presence in Mexico through the apparitions of Our Lady of Guadalupe. She made Juan Diego her ambassador to the bishop, showing us once again that God hears the cry of the poor and of those who seek the light of the gospel in the dark moments of life. Although we are of many races, languages and nations, let us celebrate our faith in Jesus Christ as one people. May devotion to Mary, the Mother of God, have a place in our hearts and in each culture represented in this house of God.

Opening Song: "Buenos días paloma blanca"

All light their candles from the paschal candle as the procession enters the church. Once inside, the ministers take their designated places, and the paschal candle is placed near the image of Our Lady of Guadalupe, wherever it is located in the church.

Prayer

> *Presider:*
> Let us pray.
> God of mercy,
> you placed the Americas under the special protection
>   of the Virgin Mary,
> Our Lady of Guadalupe.
> Grant that we may remain firm in our faith,
> serving our brothers and sisters in love
> and seeking the progress of our nations
> in the ways of justice and peace.
> We ask this through Christ our Lord.
> *R: Amen*

After the opening prayer, the candles are extinguished as all sit down for the reading of the story of the apparitions.

II. LECTURA DE LAS APARICIONES

En este momento toma lugar la lectura de las apariciones, fragmentada previamente en tres partes. (Para una posible fuente de lectura, vea el rito celebrando a la Virgen de Guadalupe en el hogar o en pequeñas comunidades de base, que sigue este.) Este es el momento para leer la primera parte (que puede abarcar las primeras dos apariciones). Luego de finalizar la lectura del primer segmento, a la vez que la asamblea entona el cánto, se enciende una de las velas de la corona de Adviento. Si se prefiere usar solamente el canto "La Guadalupana", habrá que cantar las estrofas en el intermedio de toda la lectura.

Canto: "Santa María del camino"

Se continúa con la lectura de la tercera aparición. Nuevamente se encenderá la segunda vela de la corona durante el canto.

Canto: "Santa María del camino"

Continuación de la lectura de la cuarta aparición.

Canto: "La Guadalupana"
Oración colecta (todos de pie)

    El que preside:
    Oremos.
    Padre de misericordia,
    que has puesto a este pueblo tuyo
    bajo la protección especial de la siempre Virgen María
    de Guadalupe, Madre de tu Hijo,
    concédenos, por su intercesión, profundizar en nuestra fe
    y buscar el crecimiento de nuestra comunidad
    por caminos de justicia y de paz.
    Por nuestro Señor Jesucristo.
    R: Amén

II. THE STORY OF THE APPARITIONS

The reading of the story of the apparitions follows, divided into three seg-ments. (For one possible source for the reading, see the rite celebrating Guadalupe in households or small communities that follows this one.) The first segment, which includes the account of the first two apparitions, is read at this time. Following the reading, one of the candles of the Advent wreath may be lit while all sing the song. If the song "La Guadalupana" is preferred, the verses should be sung between the readings.

Song: "Santa María del camino"

The reading of the second segment follows, which relates the story of the third apparition. Following the reading, the second candle of the Advent wreath may be lit during the song.

Song: "Santa María del camino"

The reading continues with the third segment, the story of the fourth apparition. A song follows the reading.

Song: "La Guadalupana"

Prayer (all stand)

   Presider:

   Let us pray.

   God of mercy,

   you placed this people under the special protection

   of the Ever-Virgin Mary of Guadalupe, Mother of your Son.

   Through her intercession, deepen our faith

   and help us to seek the growth of our community

   in the ways of justice and peace.

   We ask this through Christ our Lord.

   R: Amen

III. LITURGIA DE LA PALABRA

Lectura: Isaías 9:1–3 *o* Isaías 52:7–10

Aclamación antes del Evangelio
Sube aun alto monte, alegre mensajero de Jerusalén, di a las ciudades de
Judá: "¡Aquí está su Dios!" Como un pastor pastorea a su pueblo.

Evangelio: Lucas 1:39–48

Reflexión
*La reflexión podrá estar a cargo del que preside o de algún miembro de la
comunidad.*

Intercesiones generales
El diácono o uno de los ministros leerá las intercesiones.

> *El que preside:*
> Hermanos y hermanas, presentemos ahora nuestras peticiones.
>
> *Diácono u otro ministro:*
> Por la Iglesia, para que Dios nuestro Señor, quien siempre está
> del lado de los pobres, la santifique en la verdad y le sea siempre
> fiel a su fundador: Roguemos al Señor.
> *R:* Que tu santa Madre, Señor, interceda por nosotros.
> Por el Papa y los obispos, para que sean fieles al Evangelio y
> guíen a la Iglesia por el camino de la justicia y la paz: Roguemos
> al Señor.
> *R:* Que tu santa Madre, Señor, interceda por nosotros.
> Por los pueblos indígenas que sufren de opresión por parte de
> los terratenientes y los gobiernos injustos, para que sus derechos
> se reivindiquen y su dignidad sea respetada: Roguemos al Señor.
> *R:* Que tu santa Madre, Señor, interceda por nosotros.

III. LITURGY OF THE WORD

Reading: Isaiah 9:1–3 *or* Isaiah 52:7–10

Gospel Acclamation
Go up to a high mountain, Jerusalem, herald of good tidings! Say to the cities of Judah: Here is your God! The Lord will feed the chosen flock like a shepherd.

Gospel: Luke 1:39–48

Reflection
The reflection may be given by the presider or by another member of the community.

General Intercessions
The deacon or one of the ministers reads the intercessions.

Presider:
Brothers and sisters, let us now present our petitions.

Deacon or other minister:
For the church, that the Lord our God, who always hears the cry of the poor, may bless it with the truth and keep it faithful to its founder: We pray to the Lord.
R: Lord, may your holy Mother intercede for us.
For the pope and the bishops, that they may be faithful to the gospel and guide the church in the ways of justice and peace: We pray to the Lord.
R: Lord, may your holy Mother intercede for us.
For indigenous people who are discriminated against, marginalized and oppressed, that their human dignity may be respected and their civil and cultural rights defended: We pray to the Lord.
R: Lord, may your holy Mother intercede for us.

Por los inmigrantes de este país, para que sientan en Dios, la Virgen y en nuestra comunidad, una protección continua: Roguemos al Señor.

R: Que tu santa Madre, Señor, interceda por nosotros.

Por los pobres, por las personas que viven solas y lejos de sus hogares, para que a través del amor maternal de la Santísima Virgen y de nuestra presencia, sientan que Dios camina con ellos: Roguemos al Señor.

R: Que tu santa Madre, Señor, interceda por nosotros.

Por los miembros de nuestra comunidad que descansan en la paz de Dios, para que alcancen el gozo eterno de la salvación: Roguemos al Señor.

R: Que tu santa Madre, Señor, interceda por nosotros.

El que preside: Ahora cantemos juntos la oración que nos hace hermanos y hermanas:

Padre Nuestro . . .

Oración colecta

El que preside:

Oremos.

Dios de misericordia y amor,

te pedimos que por la palabra

de salvación que hemos escuchado,

alcancemos siempre la riqueza de tus dones,

y que quienes hemos participado de esta fiesta

de la Madre de Dios, bajo su advocación de

Nuestra Señora de Guadalupe,

seamos salvados por la encarnación de tu Hijo Jesucristo,

nuestro Señor, que vive y reina contigo,

por los siglos de los siglos.

R: Amén

For immigrants to this country, that they may feel the sustaining and protective embrace of God, the Virgin Mary and our community: We pray to the Lord.

R: Lord, may your holy Mother intercede for us.

For the poor, for persons who live alone and for migrants, that through the maternal love of the Virgin Mary and through our witness, they may feel that God walks with them: We pray to the Lord.

R: Lord, may your holy Mother intercede for us.

For all those of our community who rest in the peace of God, that they may enter into the joy of eternal life. We pray to the Lord.

R: Lord, may your holy Mother intercede for us.

Presider: Let us now sing together the prayer that makes us brothers and sisters:

Our Father . . .

Prayer

Presider:

Let us pray.

Merciful God,

may the words of salvation that we have heard,

always bring us the richness of your gifts.

May we who have celebrated this feast of the Mother of God,

Our Lady of Guadalupe,

be saved through the incarnation of your Son,

Jesus Christ, our Lord, who lives and reigns for ever and ever.

R: Amen.

IV. BENDICIÓN

Él que preside recitará la siguiente bendición.

Que el Señor nos bendiga, nos guarde de todo mal, y nos lleve a la vida eterna.

R: Amén.

Se puede entonar un canto mariano de despedida.

IV. BLESSING

The presider uses the following blessing.

May the Lord bless us, protect us from all evil, and bring us to everlasting life.

R. Amen.

A Marian hymn may be sung.

~❧~

Celebrando Guadalupe en casa o en Comunidades Eclesiales de Base

Este sería un momento ideal para compartir experiencias de fe, de favores recibidos de la santísima Virgen bajo su advocación de Guadalupe.

La celebración puede hacerse alrededor de un altar casero o en la mesa donde ordinariamente se comparten los alimentos. Esto podrá prepararse con anterioridad a la celebración, misma a la que pueden invitar a personas allegadas a la familia.

El que preside: Por la señal de la santa cruz, de nuestros enemigos, líbranos Señor, Dios nuestro: En el nombre del Padre, del Hijo y del Espíritu Santo.

R: Amén.

El que preside: Mi corazón en amarte, eternamente se ocupe,

R: Y mi lengua en alabarte, madre mía de Guadalupe.

El que preside: Estamos reunidos como familia de fe, formada por el amor de Dios, formada por nuestra tradición de amor a su santísima Madre, Nuestra Señora de Guadalupe, Madre de toda esperanza, Señora del Adviento, ejemplo de espera y atención a los demás. Como familia celebramos nuestra fe, esa fe que es nuestro tesoro y que nos alegra en medio de nuestras tristezas, problemas y desafíos.

Canto: "Santa María del camino"

Lectura: Eclesiástico (Sirácide) 24: 23–31

Para este momento se puede alternar la lectura de las apariciones del Nicán Mopohua *con algunas estrofas del canto "La Guadalupana". El* Nicán Mopohua *es el documento más antiguo que narra la historia de las apariciones de Nuestra Señora de Guadalupe a Juan Diego. Fue escrito en Náhuatl por Don Antonio Valeriano, escritor y académico náhuatl del siglo dieciseis. Para una referencia a las lecturas de las apariciones, vea el capítulo de la bibliografía.*

Celebrating Guadalupe in Households or Small Base Communities

Today's celebration provides a good opportunity for those present to share some of their experiences of faith and the favors received through the intercession of Our Lady of Guadalupe.

The ritual that follows may take place around a home altar or around the family dinner table, which should be decorated as desired before the celebration begins. An invitation should be extended to relatives and other friends of the family.

Presider: By the sign of the cross, free us, Lord, from our enemies: In the name of the Father, and of the Son, and of the Holy Spirit.
R: Amen.

Presider: May my heart ever love you,
R: And my tongue ever praise you, O Lady of Guadalupe.

Presider: We gather as a family of faith, formed by the love of God and by our tradition of love for the Mother of God, Our Lady of Guadalupe, Mother of all hope, Our Lady of Advent, example of confidence and loving concern for others. As a family we celebrate the treasure of our faith, a faith that uplifts and delights us in the midst of our sorrows, problems and struggles.

Song: "Santa María del camino"

Reading: Sirach 24:23–31

The story of the apparitions taken from the Nicán Mopohua *is now read. The* Nicán Mopohua *is the oldest document that tells the story of the apparitions of Our Lady of Guadalupe to Juan Diego. It was written in Náhuatl, the language of the native Mexicans, by Don Antonio Valeriano, a Náhuatl scholar of the sixteenth century. For further references to accounts of the apparitions, please see the bibliography. Refrains from the song "La Guadalupana" may be sung between the readings.*

Canto: "La Guadalupana"

Desde el cielo una hermosa mañana (2),

la guadalupana, la guadalupana,

la guadalupana, bajó al Tepeyac (2).

Lectura del libro del Nicán Mopohua

"Era sábado, muy de madrugada, y venía en pos del culto divino y de
sus mandatos. Al llegar junto al cerrillo llamado Tepeyácac amanecía y
oyó cantar arriba del cerrillo: semejaba canto de varios pájaros preciosos;
callaban a ratos las voces de los cantores; y parecía que el monte les
respondía. Su canto, muy suave y deleitoso, sobrepujaba al del COYOL-
TOTOTL y el del TZINIZCÁN y de otros pájaros lindos que cantan. Se
paró Juan Diego a ver y dijo para sí: '¿Por ventura soy digno de lo que
oigo? ¿quizá sueño? ¿me levanto de dormir? ¿dónde estoy? ¿acaso en el
paraíso terrenal, que dejaron dicho los viejos, nuestros mayores? ¿acaso
ya en el cielo?'. Estaba viendo hacia el oriente, arriba del cerrillo de
donde procedía el precioso canto celestial y así que cesó repentinamente
y se hizo el silencio, oyó que le llamaban arriba del cerrillo y le decían:
'Juanito, Juan Dieguito'".

Canto

Su llegada llenó de alegría (2),

de luz y armonía, de luz y armonía

de luz y armonía todo el Anáhuac (2).

"'Sabe y ten entendido, tú el más pequeño de mis hijos, que yo soy la
siempre Virgen Santa María, Madre del verdadero Dios por quien se

Song: "La Guadalupana"

Desde el cielo una hermosa mañana (2),

la guadalupana, la guadalupana,

la guadalupana, bajó al Tepeyac (2).

A reading from the Nicán Mopohua

"It was Saturday, when it was still night. He was going in search of the things of God and of God's messages. And when he arrived at the side of the small hill, which was named Tepeyac, it was already beginning to dawn.

"He heard singing on the summit of the hill: as if different precious birds were singing and their songs would alternate, as if the hill was answering them. Their song was most pleasing and very enjoyable, better than that of the *coyoltotol* or of the *tzinizcan* or of the other precious birds that sing.

"Juan Diego stopped and said to himself: 'By chance do I deserve this? Am I worthy of what I am hearing? Maybe I am dreaming? Maybe I only see this in my dreams? Where am I? Maybe I am in the land of my ancestors, of the elders, of our grandparents? In the Land of Flower, in the Earth of our flesh? Maybe over there inside of heaven?'

"His gaze was fixed on the summit of the hill, toward the direction from which the sun arises: the beautiful celestial song was coming from there to here. And when the song finally ceased, when everything was calm, he heard that he was being called from the summit of the hill. He heard: 'Dignified Juan, dignified Juan Diego.'"

Song

Su llegada llenó de alegría (2),

de luz y armonía, de luz y armonía

de luz y armonía todo el Anáhuac (2).

"'Know and be certain in your heart, my most abandoned son, that I am the Ever-Virgin Holy Mary, Mother of the God of Great Truth, Téotl, of

vive; del Creador cabe quien está todo; Señor del cielo y de la tierra. Deseo vivamente que se me erija aquí un templo para en él mostrar y dar todo mi amor, compasión, auxilio y defensa, pues yo soy vuestra piadosa madre; a ti, a todos vosotros juntos, los moradores de esta tierra y a los demás amadores míos que me invoquen y en mí confíen; oír allí sus lamentos, y remediar todas sus miserias, penas y dolores.

"'Y para realizar lo que mi clemencia pretende, ve al palacio del obispo de México y le dirás cómo yo te envío a manifestarle lo mucho que deseo, que aquí en el llano me edifique un templo: le contarás puntualmente cuanto has visto y admirado y lo que has oído'".

Canto
Junto al monte pasaba Juan Diego (2),
y acercose luego, y acercose luego,
y acercose luego al oír cantar (2).

"'Comprendí perfectamente en la manera como me respondió, que piensa que es quizás invención mía que Tú quieres que aquí te hagan un templo y que acaso no es de orden tuya; por lo cual te ruego encarecidamente, Señora y Niña mía, que a alguno de los principales, conocido, respetado y estimado le encargues que lleve tu mensaje para que le crean porque yo soy un hombrecillo, soy un cordel, soy una escalerilla de tablas, soy cola, soy hoja, soy gente menuda, y Tú, Niña mía, la más pequeña de mis hijas, Señora, me envías a un lugar por donde no ando y donde no paro. Perdóname que cause gran pesadumbre y caiga en tu enojo, Señora y Dueña mía'".

the One through Whom We Live, the Creator of Persons, the Owner of What Is Near and Together, of the Lord of Heaven and Earth.

"'I very much want and ardently desire that my hermitage be erected in this place. In it I will show and give to all people all my love, my compassion, my help, and my protection, because I am your merciful mother and the mother of all the nations that live on this earth who would love me, who would speak with me, who would search for me, and who would place their confidence in me. There I will hear their laments and remedy and cure all their miseries, misfortunes, and sorrows.

"'And for this merciful wish of mine to be realized, go there to the palace of the bishop of Mexico, and you will tell him in what way I have sent you as messenger, so that you may make known to him how I very much desire that he build me a home right here, that he may erect my temple on the plain. You will tell him carefully everything you have seen and admired and heard.'"

Song
Junto al monte pasaba Juan Diego (2),
y acercose luego, y acercose luego,
y acercose luego al oír cantar (2).

"'I saw perfectly, in the way he answered me, that he thinks that possibly I am just making it up that you want a temple to be built on this site, and possibly it is not your command.

"'Hence, I very much beg you, my Owner, my Queen, my Child, that you charge one of the more valuable nobles, a well-known person, one who is respected and esteemed, to come by and take your message and your word so that he may be believed. Because in reality I am one of those *campesinos*, a piece of rope, a small ladder, the excrement of people; I am a leaf; they order me around, lead me by force; and you, my most abandoned Daughter, my Child, my Lady, and my Queen, send me to a place where I do not belong. Forgive me, I will cause pain to your countenance and to your heart; I will displease you and fall under your wrath, my Lady and my Owner.'"

Canto
"Juan Dieguito", la Virgen le dijo (2),
este cerro elijo, este cerro elijo,
este cerro elijo, para ser mi altar (2).

"'Bien está, hijo mío, volverás aquí mañana para que lleves al obispo la señal que te ha pedido; con esto te creerá y acerca de esto ya no dudará ni de ti sospechará y sábete, hijito mío, que yo pagaré tu cuidado y el trabajo y cansancio que por mí has emprendido; ea vete ahora; que mañana aquí te aguardo.

"'Oye y ten entendido hijo mío el más pequeño, que es nada lo que te asusta y aflige, no se turbe tu corazón, no temas esa enfermedad, ni otra alguna enfermedad y angustia. ¿No estoy yo aquí que soy tu madre? ¿No estás bajo mi sombra? ¿No soy tu salud? ¿No estás por ventura en mi regazo? ¿Qué más has de menester? No te apene ni te inquiete otra cosa; no te aflija la enfermedad de tu tío, que no morirá ahora de ella: está seguro de que ya sanó.

"'Sube, hijo mío el más pequeño, a la cumbre del cerrillo, allí donde me viste y te di órdenes, hallarás que hay diferentes flores; córtalas, júntalas, recógelas; en seguida baja y tráelas a mi presencia. Hijo mío el más pequeño, esta diversidad de rosas es la prueba y señal que llevarás al obispo. Le dirás en mi nombre que vea en ella mi voluntad y que él tiene que cumplirla'".

Canto
Y en la tilma entre rosas pintada (2),
su imagen amada, su imagen amada,
su imagen amada se dignó dejar (2).

Song
"Juan Dieguito", la Virgen le dijo (2),
este cerro elijo, este cerro elijo,
este cerro elijo, para ser mi altar (2).

" 'My child, you shall return here tomorrow that you may take to the bishop the sign that he has asked of you. With that, he shall believe you and will no longer have any doubts or remain suspicious of you. Know that I shall repay you for the efforts you have expended on my behalf. Go now; I shall await your arrival here tomorrow.

" 'Listen and hear well in your heart, my most abandoned son: that which scares you and troubles you is nothing; do not let your countenance and heart be troubled; do not fear that sickness or any other sickness or anxiety. Am I not here, your mother? Are you not under my shadow and my protection? Am I not your source of life? Are you not in the hollow of my mantle where I cross my arms? Who else do you need? Let nothing trouble you or cause you sorrow. Do not worry because of your uncle's sickness. He will not die of his present sickness. Be assured in your heart that he is already healed.

" 'Go up, my most abandoned son, to the top of the hill, and there, where you saw me and I gave you my instructions, there you will see many diverse flowers: cut them, gather them, put them together. Then come down here and bring them before me.

" 'My most abandoned son, these different flowers are the proof, the sign, that you will take to the bishop. In my name tell him that he is to see in them what I want, and with this he should carry out my wish and my will.' "

Song
Y en la tilma entre rosas pintada (2),
su imagen amada, su imagen amada,
su imagen amada se dignó dejar (2).

"Desenvolvió luego su blanca manta, pues tenía en su regazo las flores; y así que se esparcieron por el suelo todas las diferentes rosas de Castilla, se dibujó en ella y apreció de repente la preciosa imagen de la siempre Virgen Santa María, Madre de Dios, de la manera que está y se guarda hoy en su templo del Tepeyácac, que se nombra Guadalupe".

Canto
En sus penas se postra de hinojos (2),
y eleva sus ojos, y eleva sus ojos,
y eleva sus ojos hacia el Tepeyac (2).

Intercesiones generales
Las intercesiones pueden ser de carácter espontáneo. La respuesta a ellas puede ser Que tu santa Madre, Señor, interceda por nosotros, *o alguna otra que la familia prefiera. Después, puede darse paso a las prácticas devocionales propias de cada familia.*

El que preside: Fieles a la fe que hemos recibido como regalo de Dios, fieles a su amor y a la protección maternal de su santísima Madre, recemos juntos la oración que nos hace hermanos y hermanas:

Padre Nuestro . . .

Bendición
Para este momento de la bendición, sería ideal dar preferencia a la persona de mayor edad que se encuentre en ese momento, de la manera que acostumbre hacerlo.

El que preside: Nos ofrecemos un abrazo de paz.

"He unfolded his white mantle, the mantle in whose hollow he had gathered the flowers he had cut, and at that instant the different flowers from Castile fell to the ground. In that very moment she painted herself: the precious image of the Ever-Virgin Holy Mary, Mother of the God Téotl, appeared suddenly, just as she is today and is kept in her precious home, in her hermitage of Tepeyac, which is called Guadalupe."

Song

En sus penas se postra de hinojos (2),
y eleva sus ojos, y eleva sus ojos,
y eleva sus ojos hacia el Tepeyac (2).

General Intercessions

The intercessions are spontaneous. Those present may use the following or similar response: Lord, may your holy Mother intercede for us. *At the conclusion of the intercessions an opportunity may be provided for the personal devotions of each family present.*

> *Presider:* United in the faith and love we have received as gifts from God, and in the maternal protection of the Mother of God, let us pray now together the prayer that makes us brothers and sisters:
>
> Our Father . . .

Blessing

The most senior person present may be invited to lead a spontaneous blessing.

> *Presider:* Let us offer each other a sign of peace.

꧁ ꧂

Questions for Reflection

1. *How do you teach your children and young people to prepare themselves to celebrate the Christmas season? What stories bring Christmas to life for you?*

2. *What are the cultural Advent preparations of your parish community?*

3. *What family gatherings help you prepare yourself for the celebration of Christ's birth?*

4. *What family customs prior to Christmas remind you of your heritage? Do you still practice these customs in your family today? If so, why? If not, why not?*

꧁ ꧂

1. *¿De que manera educas o enseñas a tus niños y jóvenes a prepararse a celebrar las fiestas navideñas? ¿Cuáles historias o cuentos avivan esta experiencia navideña en ti?*

2. *¿Cuáles son los preparativos culturales de Adviento que se realizan en tu parroquia?*

3. *¿Cuáles reuniones familiares te ayudan para prepararte de una mejor manera a celebrar el nacimiento de Cristo?*

4. *¿Cuáles costumbres anteriores a la Navidad te hacen recordar tu experiencia familiar? ¿Aún practicas esas costumbres en tu familia? ¿Sí? ¿No? ¿Por qué?*

Christmas

S mells evoked flavors and stirred memories of other Christmases. Mamá Pachita continued to put the finishing touches on the family's Christmas Eve meal. Papá Ramón was dozing in the front room, relaxing before the onslaught of the evening events. The meal was the centerpiece of Christmas, and it progressed gradually. Participating in the celebration was like rereading a good story. Its characters were the family members, its theme, the journey of their lives up to this very moment. Every year Christmas Eve was different, yet the same. Every year each person was different, yet the same.

Rutilio, Silvia, Lola and Chino had already left for the 9:00 PM parish family Mass at San Martín. Two years ago the base communities had asked that the time of the Midnight Mass be changed in order to accommodate families who wanted more time for their home celebrations. One great Mass at an earlier hour could bring all of their Advent preparations into the church, around their parish family table. After Mass the families would go home to meals and activities shaped by each of their traditions. Chino had also brought up a practical aspect: Unfortunately, going to and from Midnight Mass was dangerous, since drunk drivers and random gang violence took no holiday. His comment had brought an end to the discussion.

The Christmas Eve family Mass celebrated the parish family. It focused on the Christ Child and on the children of the parish. Children took on a greater role in the liturgy—in the *posada* entrance rite, the dramatization of the Christmas gospel, the blessing of each family's *Niño Dios,* and the kissing of the parish manger's *Niño Dios.* Because children belong to many worlds at the same time, crossing between the imaginary and the real with ease, the children of San Martín linked its cultures in a special way. They were natural bridge builders, motivating their parents not only to get along but to learn more about others.

The Advent celebrations of the different ethnic groups had prepared everyone for this Mass. They had expressed their faith through the experience of their distinct traditions, and through them they had become living gifts for one another.

When the family and invited friends returned from Mass, the hot fruit punch would warm them. Two of the youngest members of the family would then play central roles in the laying of the Christ Child in the crib, the *acostamiento del Niño Dios.* As *padrinos* for the *Niño Jesús,* they would rock the baby in one of Mamá Pachita's *rebozos* (shawls) while the family sang Christmas hymns. Afterward they would place the child in the family's *nacimiento* (crèche). Then, with great pride, the young *padrinos* would carry to everyone the special plate used only for this occasion, heaped with candy. The Child's presence sweetened life and brought them peace.

Mamá Pachita and Papá Ramón had decided this year that they would stay at home Christmas Eve, making the last minute preparations for the Christmas Eve meal. There was no great need to do this, the family had argued. The elderly couple knew this, but their years had caught up with them. They were tired and would rather attend Mass on Christmas morning. The family would change its custom. Mamá Pachita stirred the boiling pot of *ponche,* reflecting on the wisdom of this decision. These quiet moments settled her thoughts. She pondered her family's life as an enduring circle of transformation. The family was rehearsing for a time when she and her husband would be memories recalled at future Christmas Eve meals.

Pastoral Notes

Human Festivity and Food

Human festivity and solidarity are naturally associated with food. They serve as a way of bringing about "communion" in its most basic meaning. From the Latin *cum munire* (*cum* = "with," *munire* = "to strengthen"), the word "communion" suggests that eating together is a way of nourishing not only the body but also one's human identity as a family member within a particular culture. For this reason tradition is crucial. Eating certain foods at certain times of the year helps join those at table to each other and to their culture. It also reaffirms a bond with ancestors, both those long dead and the recently deceased, who once prepared the same holiday dishes. The link to these ancestors through food is sacred. It naturally gives rise to memories and stories of holidays past and of the people who made them so special.

_____ ᴧᴧᴧ _____

The social and cultural importance of holiday food should not be underestimated. In the North American context, what would Christmas or Thanksgiving be without turkey and pumpkin or mincemeat pie? As with other cultural groups, food and Christmas are inextricably connected in the Latino community.

The many *platillos típicos* (typical dishes) of Christmastime reflect the wonderful diversity of the Hispanic community. Not surprisingly, since Christmas is the most festive time of the year, each cultural group has developed a wide variety of dishes, from turkey stuffed with almonds (Mexico) to suckling pig (Cuba, Puerto Rico) and the various national and regional recipes for tamales, all of which are synonymous with Christmas in particular Latino cultures. Sometimes recipes must be adapted when ingredients are not available in North America, but at Christmastime Hispanic cooks try to be as faithful as possible to tradition.

The *cena,* or supper, of *Nochebuena* (Christmas Eve) is often the most important of the many festive meals during the season. At this time the extended family gathers and celebrates many of the domestic religious customs associated with Christmas: *aguinaldos* (Christmas gifts), *nacimientos* or *pesebres* (the Christmas crèche), the *arrullo* and *acostamiento del Niño Dios* (the lullaby and the laying of the infant Jesus in the crib). It is a custom in parts of Mexico and Central America to offer petitions before the Christmas Eve meal, aloud or silently, praying for the special intentions of the family. It is also customary that members of the family embrace before sitting down at table as a sign of love and reconciliation.

Linking some of these customs with the gathering of the parish family in the church will help ground the liturgical celebrations in the particular cultural genius of the people. The rites performed in Hispanic homes and neighborhoods are as organic and informal as they are devout. Words to songs and prayers have been learned by heart through years of experience, giving these observances a spontaneous and intimate feel somewhat different from the more formal church celebrations. Nevertheless, similar themes and ritual structures can reverberate in both settings.

What Time Is Midnight Mass?

Many of the Christmas customs brought to this country by people from Latin America originated in small villages (as did customs from other cultures). In a simpler, safer time and in a warmer climate, celebrating Christmas Midnight Mass (*Misa de gallo*) was a relatively easy thing to do. Family members and friends usually all lived within blocks of one another. Even when someone lived in the next village, bad weather rarely impeded their travel. In that environment, urban crime, parking congestion and long trips to visit relatives were practically unknown.

But such ideal conditions are rare now. In many large U.S. cities, parishes have begun to celebrate Christmas Eve Mass several times in order to accommodate those who feel insecure at night on city streets, especially older people. Depending on relations among cultural and linguistic groups in the parish, multicultural parishes often celebrate several Christmas Eve Masses in different languages. Changed conditions have led to changed customs. As we saw in the vignette, the traditional *Misa de gallo* at midnight has been replaced by another practice. It is now relatively common for Hispanic families of many backgrounds to gather first in the church for Christmas Mass and then in the home for supper and exchange of gifts. Parishes need to be aware of Hispanic Christmas customs observed in the home, since the church celebration will now be serving as the beginning of these festivities, not the end, as it has traditionally functioned.

The Importance of Drama in Church and at Home

A truly Latino celebration of Christmas Eve Mass will be attentive to the dramatic elements that play such an important part in celebrating this season. Happily, these customs lend themselves well to the participation of all—especially children. They also have the potential for involving people of other cultures in a multicultural celebration. Two elements from Latino tradition could be easily incorporated into the celebration of Mass: the final *posada* and the *acostamiento del Niño Dios.*

The final, abbreviated *posada* is celebrated as a way of beginning Mass with a dramatic reenactment of Mary and Joseph's search for lodging. If the assembly is too large to gather at the entrance of the church for the drama, the action could take place at a mock doorway placed in the center of the main aisle. In this scenario, the procession of priest, acolytes and other liturgical ministers stations itself in the "interior" of the church, or on the sanctuary side of the specially constructed doorway. Facing them on the other side of the doorway are a young couple dressed as Mary and Joseph with the assembly crowded behind them. After an audible knock on the door, the celebration begins with the initial posada dialogue, in which Joseph sings, *"En el nombre de cielo, os pido posada"* ("In the name of heaven I ask you for lodging"). This traditional song would be immediately familiar to most in the assembly. While the priest plays the role of the innkeeper, the whole assembly welcomes Mary and Joseph in song. For that reason the verses of the *posada* that enact Mary and Joseph's rejection are abbreviated on Christmas Eve. After only two verses of the innkeeper's refusal, the assembly responds with the bidding verse *"Entren santos peregrinos"* ("Come in, holy pilgrims") and the procession proceeds.

If it is not possible for the whole assembly to take part in the procession into the church, care should be taken to include in the procession representatives of the parish, especially children, to accompany Mary and Joseph as the welcoming verses are sung. Once the procession reaches the front of the church, Mary and Joseph take their places near the presider for the liturgy of the word. Others in the procession proceed to their seats.

As the gospel (Luke's infancy narrative) is proclaimed, the events of Christ's birth are mimed, with members of the parish— especially children—taking the parts of the shepherds and angels. This is a version of a *pastorela,* which will be discussed in more detail in the next chapter. At the end of Mass, in an action similar to the veneration of the cross on Good Friday, it is traditional in many parishes for families to come forward to venerate the statue of the *Santo Niño* with a kiss. Mary and Joseph hold the Christ Child figure as all come forward singing a *villancico* (Christmas carol). Children are especially eager to participate. It is also traditional that after kissing the statue of the Christ Child, everyone be given a piece of candy to represent the sweetness that Jesus' birth has brought to our lives.

Linking Liturgy with Home

Upon returning home, everyone is customarily served the famous *ponche,* and this is also the time for the *arrullo,* or lullaby, and the *acostamiento,* or putting to bed, to take place. The rosary begins this celebration. Then two children, a boy and a girl, may act as *padrinos* of the *acostamiento,* "presiding" at the remainder of this home rite. All can sing the *arrullo* to the Christ Child while the *padrinos* rock the figure in a *rebozo,* or shawl. After the singing, the children place the baby in the manger. Now the family makes last-minute preparations for the *Nochebuena* meal.

The Latino *nacimiento,* or home crèche, is much more elaborate than its simpler *norteño* cousin. Often, a contemporary-looking village or city surrounds the stable where the Holy Family figures are placed. It is not unusual to see busy street scenes with shops of all kinds, brightly colored buses and a veritable crowd of people going about their business. The theological statement made by this is, of course, that the birth of Christ is not simply a historical event that took place 2,000 years ago. The incarnation continues to take place here and now, in our own towns and neighborhoods.

The tradition of *intenciones,* or petitions, prior to the meal reflects the important role of reconciliation in the celebration of Christmas in Hispanic culture. Everyone present, aloud or silently, expresses an intention for the family for the coming year. Just as the *nacimiento* locates Christ's birth in the context of the here and now, so the practice of *intenciones* helps bring home the deeper meaning of the holiday. Christmas, with its family traditions and high drama, provides the perfect time for everyone to pray for the family, for loved ones, for unity and peace.

The family customs of other groups in the parish could enrich these traditional Latino Christmas practices. The Polish *oplatek,* or large host-like wafer, could be shared in the Polish fashion. Each person present breaks off a piece of this wafer, blessed in church at the end of the Christmas Eve Mass, and voices or prays silently a petition. This link with both the Christian assembly and the eucharist is striking and fits well with the tradition of *intenciones.*

A Note on Secularization

Hispanic Christmas customs, like the customs of other cultural groups, are under increasing pressure from the larger society to conform to the prevailing secular view of Christmas. Unlike Thanksgiving, which has retained its links to family and domestic celebration, Christmas is largely a consumer holiday in secular North American culture, promoted by advertising and commercial interests that benefit financially by emphasizing gift-giving and Santa Claus over the incarnation of Christ and reconciliation. In a consumer-dominated culture there is little left to celebrate after the purchase and exchange of gifts. Christmas quickly fades after December 25.

In parts of Latin America as well, there is a tendency to use Christmas as just another excuse for a good party. *"Disco-posadas"* are a recent phenomenon in Mexico. They are not an opportunity to pray and celebrate the coming birth of Christ but to dance and party. While modern culture inevitably affects religious practice, pastoral leaders can continue to promote the traditional (and countercultural) vision of Christmas. Hispanic popular religious customs, as well as those of other ethnic groups, practiced in church and in the home can emphasize both the holiness and the festivity of Christmas.

Posada de Nochebuena para el rito de entrada de la Misa

Es el último día para pedir posada. La procesión tomará lugar desde la casa que los recibió por última vez hasta llegar a la puerta de la iglesia. Se asume que los peregrinos vendrán acompañados por la familia que los recibió así como los demás miembros de la comunidad que los acompañarán en el trayecto a la parroquia. Sería ideal que algunas de las personas que vengan acompañando a los peregrinos, se vistan al estilo judío de la época. Esto ayudará para una dramatización no verbal del Evangelio, en lo que el diácono hace la proclamación.

La iglesia estará a media luz. La gente se encuentra adentro y tendrá sus propias velas. El sacerdote, junto con el diácono o ministro, permanece a la entrada. Con la asamblea, reciben a los peregrinos. Los acompaña el coro, aunque se espera que cante toda la asamblea. El diácono u otro ministro lleva una vela de la corona de Adviento.

Habrá que acordar la hora de llegada a la iglesia, para que la petición de posada se una al rito de entrada de la celebración de Navidad. Una vez que han llegado, inician el canto para pedir posada. Junto con el canto para pedir posada, comienza la procesión, el que preside junto con los ministros y peregrinos se dirigen el frente, deteniéndose brevemente en tres ocasiones para que la asamblea pueda encender sus velas. Dichos momentos reflejan las tres pausas que se hacen con el cirio pascual durante la Vigilia Pascual.

El sacerdote: Hermanos y hermanas, esta noche es nuestro día, Dios se hizo carne y habitó entre nosotros. Recordemos su nacimiento, el cumplimiento de la promesa del Padre en Jesucristo, hecho Niño para gloria de Dios. Celebremos también nuestra tradición, dando posada a los peregrinos María y José en esta noche de gloria.

Posada Entrance Rite for Christmas Eve Mass

Christmas Eve marks the final celebration of the *posada*. The *posada* procession this evening begins at the last home visited by the statues of the pilgrims Joseph and Mary, and continues to the door of the parish church. In addition to the members of the family that last welcomed the statues of the pilgrims, other members of the parish community also join in the procession. It would be ideal if some of those taking part in the procession dress as first-century Israelites. This will enhance the non-verbal aspect of the dramatization at the time of the reading of the gospel, proclaimed by the deacon.

The church is in semidarkness, and the assembly is seated inside. Each person has his or her own candle. The presider and other liturgical ministers stand inside the door of the church. With the assembly, they play the role of the innkeeper. The choir accompanies them, although it is hoped that the entire assembly would join in the singing. The deacon or other minister holds a lit candle from the Advent wreath.

The posada *procession will need to be timed so as to arrive at the church at the beginning of the Christmas Eve Mass and become part of the entrance rite. Once the procession arrives, the pilgrims begin the* posada *song, asking for lodging. The procession of liturgical ministers and pilgrims moves into the church as three verses of the song are sung, pausing three times so that the assembly can light their candles. The lights in the church are turned on gradually during these three stages, recalling the three-stage entrance of the paschal candle during the Easter Vigil.*

Presider: My brothers and sisters, this night is like the day for us. Our God became flesh and lived among us. Let us recall the birth of Jesus Christ, the fulfillment of the promise of the Father. Let us also celebrate our tradition, giving lodging to the pilgrims Mary and Joseph on this glorious night.

Fuera
En el nombre del cielo
os pido posada
pues no puede andar
mi esposa amada.

Respuesta
Aquí no es mesón,
sigan adelante,
yo no puedo abrir,
no sea algún tunante.

En este momento se encienden las primeras veladoras de la vela de Adviento que lleva el ministro o el diácono.

Fuera
Venimos rendidos
desde Nazaret.
Yo soy carpintero
de nombre José.

Respuesta
No me importa el nombre,
déjenme dormir,
pues que ya les digo
que no hemos de abrir.

Se encienden más veladoras dentro de la iglesia.

It is recommended that the posada *song be sung in Spanish. The following translation will help non–Spanish-speaking participants to understand the* posada *dialogue.*

> *Outside*
> In the name of heaven
> I ask you for lodging,
> because to keep on going
> my beloved wife is unable.
>
> *Reply*
> This is not an inn;
> continue on your way;
> I can't open [the door];
> you may be riffraff.

At this point some members of the assembly light their candles from the Advent candle carried by the minister or deacon.

> *Outside*
> We are very tired,
> coming from Nazareth.
> I am a carpenter,
> Joseph by name.
>
> *Reply*
> I don't care about your name;
> let me sleep;
> I already told you
> that we're not going to open.

More members of the assembly light their candles inside the church.

Fuera
Mi esposa es María,
es Reina del Cielo,
y madre va a ser
del Divino Verbo.

Respuesta
¿Eres tú José?
¿Tu esposa es María?
Entren peregrinos,
no los conocía.

Al terminar el canto, se prenden todas las velas de la iglesia, las de la asamblea y todo el conjunto de luces que esté disponible. Una vez que todos los ministros y los peregrinos están en el presbiterio, cada quien tomará su lugar respectivo y juntos cantarán:

Humildes peregrinos, Jesús, María y José (2),
mi alma os doy, mi alma os doy, y con ella
mi corazón también (2).

El diácono o ministro remplaza la vela en la corona de Adviento. La celebración continúa con el canto del Gloria. A partir de este momento, la Misa continúa.

Outside
My wife is Mary,
she is the Queen of Heaven,
and she is going to be mother
of the Divine Word.

Reply
Are you Joseph?
Your wife is Mary?
Come in, pilgrims,
I did not know who you were.

At the conclusion of the song, the rest of the candles in the church are lit, and all other available lights are turned on. Once all the ministers and the pilgrims are in the sanctuary, they each take their respective places and sing together (in Spanish):

Humble pilgrims: Jesus, Mary and Joseph (2),
I give you my soul, I give you my soul, and with it
    my heart as well (2).

The deacon or minister replaces the candle in the Advent wreath. The celebration continues with the singing of the Gloria. Then the Mass for Christmas Eve continues.

Posada en el barrio de San Martín de Porres

Este es un rito para la última noche del novenario de las posadas si la comunidad no está celebrando el ultimo día de la Posada en la iglesia. Este mismo modelo puede seguirse para cada uno de los días de la novena, utilizando las lecturas de Adviento u otras más tradicionales. Tomando eso en cuenta, es importante hacer la conexión de la celebración de hoy, con lo que ya se avecina, el nacimiento del Hijo de Dios.

La procesión con los Santos Peregrinos habrá que hacerla de la casa que ha hospedado a los peregrinos la noche anterior, hasta el hogar donde serán hospedados. Es conveniente la variación en cuanto a las personas que llevarán los peregrinos. Ayudará el que estos se coloquen en una tarima firme que permitan que las personas los lleven sobre sus hombros. Una vez que llegan a la casa donde pasarán la noche los Santos Peregrinos, si el clima lo permite, el grupo puede rezar el rosario y luego dividirse en dos y pedir posada.

Se debe proveer suficientes copias con los cantos necesarios para la celebración, así como las veladoras que llevarán los participantes en la procesión. El coro desarrollará mejor su función si se coloca en medio de la gente, para que así pueda acompañar mejor a los participantes.

Líder: Hermanos y hermanas: nos hemos reunido como una comunidad de fe, para revivir la historia de nuestra salvación, vivamos esta experiencia compartiendo con José y María su caminar en busca de posada. Hagámoslo pensando en las personas que aún siguen peregrinando en busca de un hogar digno para ellos y sus familias. Al mismo tiempo, celebremos nuestra tradición y la alegría de la espera del Hijo de Dios.

A partir de este momento, inicia el rezo del rosario. Entre cada misterio habrá cantos propios de las posadas, así como jaculatorias para después de cada misterio.

Posada in the Neighborhood of San Martín de Porres

This is a rite for the last night of the nine-day celebration of the *posadas* if it is not to be celebrated in the church. This model may be used for each of the nine days, using the Advent scripture readings or other, more traditional ones. Today, however, it is important to make clear the connection between the *posada* and the feast that draws near, the celebration of the birth of the Son of God.

The procession with the statues of the holy pilgrims begins at the home that offered lodging the night before, and continues to the home that offers lodging this night. Different members of the community should be invited to carry the statues each night. It is advisable that the statues be secured to a solid wooden platform that can be borne on the shoulders of those who will carry it. Upon the arrival of the holy pilgrims at the home where they will spend the night, weather permitting, the group may pray the rosary and later divide into two groups for the singing of the posada *song.*

Worship aids containing song lyrics and directions, as well as small candles, should be provided for those participating in the procession. The choir should gather among the people where it may better lead the participants in song.

> *Leader:* My brothers and sisters, gathered as a community of faith to relive the story of our salvation, let us live this experience, sharing with Mary and Joseph their search for lodging. Let us also recall those who even now are in search of a home for themselves and their families. At the same time, let us celebrate our tradition and the joy of waiting for the Son of God.

The praying of the rosary follows, which is preceded by a brief penitential prayer. Between each mystery there may be songs appropriate to the posadas, *as well as exclamatory prayers after each mystery.*

Líder: Por la señal de la santa cruz, de nuestros enemigos, líbranos Señor, Dios nuestro: En el nombre del Padre, del Hijo y del Espíritu Santo.

R: Amén.

Líder: Dios mío, me arrepiento de todo corazón de haberte ofendido, porque eres infinitamente bueno. Dame tu santa gracia para no ofenderte más. Amén.

o:

Yo confieso . . .

Líder: Gloria al Padre, al Hijo y al Espíritu Santo:

R: Como era en un principio, ahora y siempre, por los siglos de los siglos. Amén.

Jaculatoria

Líder: Humildes peregrinos, Jesús, María y José:

R: Mi alma os doy y con ella mi corazón también.

Después de haber rezado el rosario, se continuará con la letanía lauretana. Una vez que ha finalizado la letanía, se termina el rosario de la forma tradicional con las siguientes oraciones o las que el pueblo acostumbre.

Líder: Bajo tu amparo nos acogemos Santa Madre de Dios, no desprecies las súplicas que te hacemos en nuestras necesidades, antes bien, líbranos de todo peligro, ¡oh! Virgen gloriosa y bendita.

R: Ruega por nosotros Santa Madre de Dios, para que seamos dignos y merecedores de alcanzar las divinas gracias y promesas de Nuestro Señor Jesucristo. Amén.

Oración de consagración a María

¡Oh! Señora mía,

¡oh! Madre mía,

yo me ofrezco enteramente a ti.

en prueba de mi filial afecto,

Leader: By the sign of the cross, free us, Lord, from our enemies: In the name of the Father, and of the Son, and of the Holy Spirit.

R: Amen.

Leader: O my God, I am heartily sorry for having offended you, because you are all good and deserving of all my love. Give me your holy grace that I might offend you no further. Amen.

or:

I confess . . .

Leader: Glory to the Father, and to the Son, and to the Holy Spirit:

R: As it was in the beginning, is now and will be for ever. Amen.

Exclamatory Prayer

Leader: To you, O humble pilgrims, Jesus, Mary and Joseph:

R: I give my soul, and with it my heart as well.

The litany of the Blessed Virgin Mary follows the praying of the rosary. After the litany, the rosary is concluded in the traditional way with the following prayers, or those more commonly used by the people.

Leader: We take refuge in you, O Holy Mother of God. Do not despise the supplications we make to you in our time of need, but free us from all danger, O blessed and glorious Virgin.

R: Pray for us, O Holy Mother of God, that we may be worthy and deserving to obtain the divine promises of our Lord Jesus Christ. Amen.

Prayer of Consecration to the Virgin Mary

O Virgin Mary,

my dearest Mother,

I offer myself completely to you.

As proof of my filial affection,

te consagro en este día, y para siempre,
mis ojos, mis oídos, mi lengua y mi corazón.
En una palabra, todo mi ser,
ya que soy todo tuyo ¡oh! Madre de bondad.
Guárdame y defiéndeme, como cosa y posesión tuya.
R: Amén.

Versos para pedir posada

Afuera

1. En el nombre del cielo
os pido posada
pues no puede andar
mi esposa amada.

2. No seas inhumano,
ténnos caridad
que el Dios de los cielos
te lo premiará.

3. Venimos rendidos
desde Nazaret.
Yo soy carpintero
de nombre José.

4. Posada te pide,
amado casero,
por solo una noche
la Reina del Cielo.

Adentro

1. Aquí no es mesón,
sigan adelante,
yo no puedo abrir,
no sea algún tunante.

2. Ya se pueden ir
y no molestar,
porque si me enfado
os voy a apalear.

3. No me importa el nombre,
déjenme dormir,
pues que ya les digo
que no hemos de abrir.

4. Pues si es una reina
quien lo solicita,
¿cómo es que de noche
anda tan solita?

I consecrate to you now and forever
my eyes, my ears, my tongue, my heart—
in a word, my entire being.
I am yours completely, O Mother of goodness.
Guard me and defend me, as you would your very self.
R: Amen.

Verses of the Posada Song
Although the posada *song will be sung in Spanish, an English translation*
is provided below.

Outside

1. In the name of heaven
I ask you for lodging,
because to keep on going
my beloved wife is unable.

2. Don't be inhuman,
have charity for us
that the God of heaven
may repay you for it.

3. We are very tired,
coming from Nazareth.
I am a carpenter,
Joseph by name.

4. Asking you for lodging,
kind homeowner,
for only one night,
is the Queen of Heaven.

Inside

1. This is not an inn;
continue on your way;
I can't open [the door];
you may be riffraff.

2. You may go now
and don't bother us,
because if I get angry
I'm going to hit you.

3. I don't care about
 your name;
let me sleep;
I already told you
that we're not going to open.

4. If she is a queen
who is asking,
how is it that at night
she is walking alone?

Afuera

5. Mi esposa es María,
es Reina del Cielo,
y madre va a ser
del Divino Verbo.

6. Dios pague, señores,
vuestra caridad,
y así os colme el cielo,
de felicidad.

Adentro

5. ¿Eres tú José?
¿Tu esposa es María?
Entren peregrinos,
no los conocía.

6. ¡Dichosa la casa
que alberga este día
a la Virgen pura,
la hermosa María!

Canto de conclusión al entrar en la casa
Todos adentro

Entren santos peregrinos, peregrinos,
reciban este rincón.
Que aunque es pobre la morada,
la morada,
os la doy de corazón.
Cantemos con alegría, alegría,
todos al considerar. Que Jesús, José y María, y María,
nos vinieron hoy a honrar (2).

Este es el momento apropiado para compartir los aguinaldos, bebidas y comidas tradicionales, al igual que las piñatas.

Outside	Inside
5. My wife is Mary, she is the Queen of Heaven, and she is going to be mother of the Divine Word.	5. Are you Joseph? Your wife is Mary? Come in, pilgrims, I did not know who you were.
6. May God reward, good persons, your charity, and may heaven fill you with happiness.	6. Happy the home that houses today the pure Virgin, the beautiful Mary!

Song for the Conclusion of the Entrance into the House

All inside

Come in, holy pilgrims, pilgrims,
accept this corner,
not of this poor house,
but of my heart.
Let us sing with joy, joy,
as we all consider
that Jesus, Joseph and Mary,
honor us today with their presence.

This is the appropriate time for sharing small gifts and traditional food and drink, as well as breaking piñatas.

Acostamiento del Niño Dios dentro de la Misa de Nochebuena

Esta es una celebración totalmente popular, por lo tanto, no existe un momento propio dentro de la Misa para hacer el acostamiento. La forma ideal en que se puede hacer, es por medio de una dramatización del Evangelio en la que participan José, María, los pastores y el ángel que anuncia el nacimiento del Hijo de Dios.

La dramatización buscará enfatizar la proclamación del Evangelio. Este estilo de dramatización crearía un espacio excelente en la participación de los niños dentro de la liturgia de Nochebuena. José y María, por su parte, acostarán al Niño en el pesebre una vez que el Evangelio lo indique. Al finalizar la proclamación del Evangelio, todos cantan el arrullo tradicional u orto canto apropiado.

Canto de arrullo

> Duerme y no llores,
>
> Jesús del alma,
>
> duerme y no llores,
>
> mi dulce amor.
>
> Duerme y no llores,
>
> que esas tus lágrimas
>
> parten el alma de compasión.

A partir de este momento, se continúa con el esquema de Misa. Luego de la bendición, mientras entonan el canto de salida y como rito de despedida, José y María se colocan el frente ofrecen el Niño Dios a la asamblea para que los que deseen, lo veneren con un beso.

Laying of the Christ Child in the Crib during Christmas Eve Mass

The laying of the Christ Child in the crib is of popular origin. There is no designated or expected time for it during the Mass. The ideal format for the laying of the Christ Child in the crib is through a dramatization of the gospel in which Joseph, Mary, the shepherds, and the angel who announces the birth of the Son of God participate.

The dramatization seeks to emphasize the proclamation of the gospel. This style of dramatization is an excellent opportunity for the participation of children during the liturgy on Christmas Eve. Joseph and Mary, for their part, lay the Christ Child in the crib according to the cues of the gospel reading. After the proclamation of the gospel, all sing the traditional lullaby (in Spanish) or another appropriate song.

Lullaby

> Sleep and don't cry,
> Jesus of my soul.
> Sleep and don't cry,
> my sweet love.
> Sleep and don't cry
> for your tears will break my heart.

Following the lullaby, Mass continues as usual. After the blessing, when the recessional song begins, Joseph and Mary come forward and offer the Christ Child for veneration.

Acostamiento del Niño Dios en casa

Tradicionalmente la familia que ha invitado al acostamiento se prepara con pinole (maíz dorado, triturado y mezclado con azúcar) y priote (dulce que se elabora con maíz y azúcar), atole, té, café, ponche, champurrado o algún otro tipo de bebida que ofrecerá a las personas que los acompañen.

El acostamiento toma lugar en donde han preparado el nacimiento. La celebración inicia con el rezo del rosario (con oraciones exclamatorias entre cada misterio), precedido por un acto de contrición, y los misterios en los que se medita ese día son gozosos.

> *Líder:* Por la señal de la santa cruz, de nuestros enemigos, líbranos Señor, Dios nuestro. En el nombre del Padre, del Hijo, y del Espíritu Santo.
> *R:* Amén.
>
> *Líder:* Dios mío, me arrepiento de todo corazón de haberte ofendido, porque eres infinitamente bueno. Dame tu santa gracia para no ofenderte más. Amén.

o:

> Yo confieso . . .
>
> *Líder:* Gloria al Padre, al Hijo y al Espíritu Santo:
> *R:* Como era en un principio, ahora y siempre, por los siglos, de los siglos. Amén.

Jaculatoria

> *Líder:* Niñito Jesús:
> *R:* Házme ver la luz.

Se entona un canto navideño o mariano entre cada misterio. El rosario continúa como de costumbre, una vez que se finaliza la letanía lauretana y las devociones que las personas acostumbran rezar, la persona que preside la celebración, realiza una oración a nombre de todos. Puede utilizarse la siguiente:

Laying of the Christ Child in the Crib at Home

The family that hosts a celebration of the *acostamiento* traditionally prepares for their guests *pinole* (ground toasted corn mixed with sugar) and *priote* (a sweet made from corn and sugar), *atole* (a cornmeal drink), tea, coffee, fruit punch, *champurrado* (a mixed drink of chocolate and atole) and other beverages.

The acostamiento *takes place at the crèche or nativity scene. The celebration begins with the praying of the joyful mysteries of the rosary (with exclamatory prayers between each mystery) and is preceded by a brief penitential prayer.*

> *Leader:* By the sign of the cross, free us, Lord, from our enemies: In the name of the Father, and of the Son, and of the Holy Spirit.
>
> *R:* Amen.
>
> *Leader:* O my God, I am heartily sorry for having offended you, because you are all good and deserving of all my love. Give me your holy grace that I might offend you no further. Amen.

or:

> I confess . . .
>
> *Leader:* Glory to the Father, and to the Son, and to the Holy Spirit:
>
> *R:* As it was in the beginning, is now and will be for ever. Amen.

> *Exclamatory Prayer*
>
> *Leader:* O little child Jesus:
>
> *R:* Make me see the light.

A Christmas or Marian song may be sung between each mystery. The rosary continues as usual. After the litany of the Blessed Virgin Mary and the customary devotions, the presider prays in the name of all. The following prayer may be used:

Líder:
Bendito sea Dios, Padre Nuestro,
que nos concede recordar
y celebrar con fe
los misterios de su Hijo.
Que él nos conceda la gracia,
para que sostenidos por la fe,
alcancemos un día,
gozar de su gloria eterna,
por Cristo nuestro Señor.
R: Amén.

La persona más adulta que esté participando, tomará el Niño Dios en sus manos, lo besará y lo arrullará un poco. Así sucesivamente cada uno de los ahí presentes. Mientras tanto, se entonan cánticos navideños o de alabanza. Una vez que todos han arrullado al Niño Dios, se coloca en el pesebre y se finaliza con alguna oración de consagración a María.

¡Oh! Señora mía,
¡oh! Madre mía,
yo me ofrezco enteramente a ti.
en prueba de mi filial afecto,
te consagro en este día, y para siempre,
mis ojos, mis oídos, mi lengua y mi corazón.
En una palabra, todo mi ser,
ya que soy todo tuyo ¡oh! Madre de bondad.
Guárdame y defiéndeme, como cosa y posesión tuya. Amén.

Leader:
Blessed are you, God our Father,
who give us this time to remember
and celebrate with faith
the mysteries of your Son.
May he grant us your grace,
so that sustained by faith
we may one day rejoice in your eternal glory,
through Christ our Lord.
R: Amen.

The most senior of those present takes the Christ Child, reverences it with a kiss, and sings a brief lullaby. All the others present then do likewise. Meanwhile, Christmas songs or hymns of praise may be sung. After all have offered their lullaby to the Christ Child, the figure is laid in the crib. The prayer concludes with a consecration to Mary.

O Virgin Mary,
my dearest Mother,
I offer myself completely to you.
As proof of my filial affection,
I consecrate to you now and forever
my eyes, my ears, my tongue, my heart—
in a word, my entire being.
I am yours completely, O Mother of goodness.
Guard me and defend me, as you would your very self. Amen.

Oración para bendecir los alimentos en Nochebuena

El carácter de la oración es muy espontáneo. La primera parte la puede hacer el papá, la segunda la mamá, la tercera alguno de los hijos. El esquema de oración puede adaptarse a la experiencia de cada familia e invitados. Se puede intercalar un canto entre cada sección.

La persona de mayor edad ahí presente: Por la señal de la santa cruz, de nuestros enemigos, líbranos Señor, Dios nuestro: En el nombre del Padre, del Hijo y del Espíritu Santo.

R: Amén.

Papá:
Señor Dios Nuestro,
creador del cielo y de la tierra,
que te hiciste uno de nosotros
en la persona de Jesús
para quedarte y darnos
una vida que no se acaba.
Te damos gracias por enviar a tu Hijo a la tierra
y con Él hacerte alimento nuestro
en la Eucaristía y en la Palabra;
en la presencia de quien vive solo y desamparado
y en el testimonio de quienes se han entregado a ti
en servicio a los demás.

Canto navideño

Mamá:
Te damos gracias Señor
por la vida que nos das a cada instante,
por llamarnos a ser parte de tu obra creadora.
Gracias por elegirnos para ser instrumentos de tu paz.
Te damos gracias por la naturaleza que nos habla de ti,

Blessing of Food on Christmas Eve

This prayer has a very spontaneous character. The first part may be led by the father, the second by the mother, the third by one of the children of the family. The order of the prayer may be adapted according to the experiences of each family and its invited friends. A song may be inserted between each section.

The eldest of those present: By the sign of the cross, free us Lord, from our enemies: In the name of the Father, and of the Son, and of the Holy Spirit.

R: Amen.

Father:
Lord our God,
creator of heaven and earth,
who became one of us in the person of Jesus
in order to provide us with life in abundance,
we give you thanks for sending your Son to earth,
for becoming our nourishment
in the eucharist and in the word,
in those who are alone and forsaken,
and in the testimony of those who have devoted
    themselves to you
in the service of others.

Christmas Song

Mother:
We give you thanks for the life
that you give us each day,
for calling us to be part of your work of creation,
for choosing us to be instruments of your peace;
we give you thanks for nature,

por el encuentro amoroso entre nuestras familias
que renueva nuestra fe y trae alegría a nuestros hogares.
Gracias porque con tu venida a la tierra y a este hogar
nos trajiste vida en abundancia.

Canto navideño
Hijo(a):

Bendice Señor nuestra mesa,
bendice nuestras manos,
bendícelas con tu generosidad
para que siempre estemos dispuestos
a compartir tus dones
con los más necesitados.
Bendice los alimentos que esta noche vamos a compartir
a fin de que renueven nuestras fuerzas
y la alegría de reunirnos en torno a la mesa.
Que el gozo de estar juntos perdure para siempre.

La persona de mayor edad ahí presente:

Te lo pedimos a Ti, Padre, con fe,
en la unidad de tu Hijo recién nacido,
y tu Santo Espíritu,
dador de vida, que nos guía y alimenta.
R: Amén.

Se puede intercambiar un signo de paz.

which speaks to us of you,

and for the love we encounter in our families,

which renews our faith

and brings happiness to our homes.

We give you thanks because through your coming to earth
	and to this home

you have brought us abundant life.

Christmas Song
Son or daughter:

Bless our table, O Lord.

Bless our hands with your generosity,

so that we may always be disposed

to share your gifts with those most in need.

Bless our meal this night;

may it renew our strength

and our happiness at being together around your table.

May the joy of being together last forever.

The eldest person present:

We ask you this, Father, with faith,

in union with your newborn Son,

and your Holy Spirit,

the giver of life, who guides and feeds us.

R: Amen.

A sign of peace may be exchanged.

　ᴥ

Questions for Reflection

1. *What family Christmas Eve customs do you remember as being significant during your childhood? What gospel themes do they reflect?*

2. *What traditional foods and meals were prepared for Christmas Eve/Day? In what way were these festive meals important to the family?*

3. *What Christmas carols were especially meaningful and memorable? Is the experience of Christmas contained in these melodies and lyrics?*

4. *Are there connections between the Christmas celebration of the local parish and your celebration at home?*

5. *What Christmas practices of other racial or ethnic groups challenge you to be more inclusive in the way you act toward them?*

ᴥ

1. *¿Cuáles costumbres navideñas de tu niñez recuerdas con un cariño especial? ¿Qué temas del Evangelio se ven reflejados en esas costumbres?*

2. *¿Qué platillos tradicionales eran los que se preparaban para la cena de Navidad? ¿En qué sentido estos alimentos eran importantes para la familia?*

3. *¿Cuáles villancicos tenían un sentido especial y recuerdas con más ahínco? ¿De qué forma estos villancicos reflejan la experiencia de la Navidad?*

4. *¿Existe alguna conexión entre la celebración de la Navidad que se celebra en tu parroquia y las celebraciones que se realizan en tu casa?*

5. *¿Qué prácticas cristianas de otros grupos étnicos te desafían a ser más inclusivo y acercarte a su cultura con nuevas actitudes?*

Christmas and Beyond

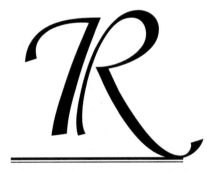utilio and Silvia lay in bed pretending to be asleep. They did not want to disturb one another. Was it their body clocks waking them before dawn, or just the anticipation that tonight after work they would celebrate the close of the Christmas season with their *compadres* in a neighbor's home? The precious moments of pretend sleep eased them into the day. They reminisced about the journey of these past few weeks.

The journey had begun when the liturgy team shared with Father John their personal experiences of Christmas as well as their visions of this year's parish celebrations. Almost all mentioned that Christmas began on *Nochebuena,* Christmas Eve, and continued until *Candelaria* on February 2. (Known as Candlemas by many of the older English-speaking people of the parish, this feast was once celebrated as the Purification of Mary but is now the feast of the Presentation of the Lord.)

The base community representatives had wanted to celebrate New Year's Eve by holding the customary Holy Hour before the Blessed Sacrament. This quiet prayer could then continue in their homes in a less formal service. The theme of the New Year's Eve prayer would be thanksgiving for the blessings received in the past year, both as a parish community and as a family, but also for what the coming year would bring. These prayer services offered everyone a chance to review parish and family life in the light of the gospel. Reminding themselves of the volatile and precarious atmosphere of New Year's Eve, the team wanted to hold the church Holy Hour from 8:00 to 9:00 PM. This would allow families to return home safely for their household prayer time and New Year's Eve parties.

Everyone had taken a minute to speak about how they looked forward to January 6 and its various celebrations, especially the *Tres Reyes Magos* gathering. Of course, various households continued with the *parrandas,* the neighborhood caroling. The parish had recently used this time around Epiphany to support needy families, both of their own neighborhoods and of the local shelter. Epiphany was also celebrated with the *rosca,* a special bread that contained little plastic figures of the Christ Child. Families would gather to share this round sweet loaf after Mass on Epiphany, and those who found the small infant in their piece of bread would become *padrinos* (sponsors) for the lifting up of the Christ Child, the *levantamiento del Niño Dios* celebration on February 2. That day was the occasion for families to bring their *Niño Dios* to the church for a final blessing. At home, after the Child was dressed in new clothes provided by the *padrinos,* he was lifted up, reverently kissed, and then put away until next year.

At the same meeting Father John had talked to them about the *comites Christi* feasts that followed Christmas. He noted that Christian tradition has long honored these "companions of Christ" as martyrs, or "witnesses." Stephen, deacon and "protomartyr" (the first martyr) (December 26), was stoned by a crowd that was incensed by his preaching about Jesus. According to popular belief, John the Evangelist (December 27) bravely risked death by drinking from a cup he knew was poisoned to demonstrate Christ's power over death. He lived to a ripe old age on the island of Patmos, where, according to tradition, he wrote the book of Revelation. (Because of his willingness to drink the poison, Saint John is often depicted holding a cup containing a serpent.) Finally, the Holy Innocents (December 28) died for Christ since it was because of Jesus and his birth in Bethlehem that Herod gave the order for the slaughter of all young male children in that locality. Unlike Stephen and John, the Holy Innocents did not choose martyrdom since they suffered death at the hands of the soldiers of the king. All of these characters of the Christmas season foreshadow Lent and Holy Week.

The word "character" reminded Rutilio of the antics of his son Chino. *Los Santos Inocentes* (December 28) is the Mexican equivalent of April Fools' Day, when jokes are played on the unsuspecting. Father John was a prime target for Chino's tricks, and throughout the day whenever Chino caught the priest in some prank, the chorus, "*¡Inocente palomita que te dejas atrapar!*" ("Innocent little dove, you let yourself get caught!") was heard throughout the rectory.

As Rutilio listened to the team's ideas develop from their initial interest in the *comites Christi* to a plan for shaping this year's *pastorelas* around *Los Santos Inocentes,* he realized that Chino's energy could be channeled into organizing the young people to present this drama as an evangelization project. To supplement Chino's high spirits and organizational gifts, the parish could rely on the local literary, musical and dramatic talent. The liturgy team's discussion had generated plans that renewed people's lives as the extended Christmas season unfolded.

Rutilio and Silvia reviewed their favorite events privately in the quiet of their pretend sleep. They knew that Christmas had been celebrated well this year. The bed creaked as Silvia made the first move and woke up the still-pretending Rutilio with a morning kiss.

Pastoral Notes

As we have already noted, for many Latinos the religious contours of the holiday season are significantly more obvious than they are for many in mainstream U.S. culture. Rather than signaling the culmination of the religious aspect of the holiday season, the Mass on Christmas Eve—*Nochebuena*—is really more like the midway point of the Advent-Christmas celebration. This period of the year is never without religious observances of some kind. It begins with the first Sunday of Advent and the pre-Christmas tradition of *posadas* and does really not end until the feast of the Presentation of the Lord *(Candelaria)* on February 2.

While Christmas carols seem a bit "worn out" after Christmas in non-Hispanic communities, the Latino capability for linking celebration to religious observance continues to find expression in dramatic and exuberant forms. Among Mexicans, *pastorelas* are plays that narrate the birth of Jesus with grace and humor. The Puerto Rican custom of house-to-house group caroling *(parrandas)* continues from Christmas to *Los Reyes Magos* (Epiphany, January 6). New Year's celebrations can assume a more religious character than in the surrounding culture, and for many Latinos Epiphany serves as the time of gift-giving and special foods. Finally, *Candelaria* (February 2) marks the end of the season, when the statue of the infant Jesus is carefully removed from the home *nacimiento* and the rest of the Christmas decorations are put away until the next Christmas.

Attending to the Traditions

During this season one of the key aspects of ministry—both liturgical and extra-liturgical—is for pastoral ministers to be aware of the range of Hispanic Christmas traditions present in the parish. In our story, Father John was wise to have asked the members of the liturgy team about their particular experiences of Christmas as a way of beginning the planning for the liturgical celebrations, since these practices serve as a backdrop and a potential enrichment for the common prayer of the parish.

Traditions also vary a great deal from group to group, so conversation about the range of traditions in the parish is always important. Such a meeting also provides the opportunity to elicit the experiences and ideas of all of the ethnic groups of the parish. Often, pastoral ministers are pleasantly surprised to see points of contact between cultures and traditions that can serve as a way of bringing together the various groups of the parish. At the very least, all groups must be taken into consideration when scheduling Masses and other events.

Pastorelas

Pastorelas are dramas that reenact the birth of Christ and can be performed in a variety of venues: churches, auditoriums or even outside if it is warm. They originated in sixteenth-century Mexico and developed out of the mystery plays of the Middle Ages in western Europe. Performed on church porches and sometimes inside the church itself, mystery plays were meant to give dramatic form to the stories of the faith. This European custom was brought to the New World by the missionaries to serve as a catechetical tool in an age when few were literate but all appreciated a good drama. Friar Andrés de Olmos is credited with having composed the first *pastorela, Adoración de los Reyes Magos.* Bishop Zumárraga, the same bishop who skeptically received Juan Diego and eventually believed in the apparition of Our Lady of Guadalupe at Tepeyac, gave approval for the performance of the first *pastorelas* in New Spain.

While loosely based on the nativity narratives found in the gospels of Luke and Matthew, *pastorelas,* like the mystery plays, deal with the cosmic significance of the birth of Christ, depicted as an epic struggle between the archangel Michael and Satan. Modern *pastorelas* focus on the struggle of the shepherds (in Spanish, *pastores,* hence *pastorelas*) to reach the infant Jesus in Bethlehem. At work in the hills, they hear the good news of the birth of Christ from the angels and begin their journey. On the road they are beset by demons lying in wait, who try to prevent them from arriving at the manger by throwing all kinds of obstacles and temptations in their way. With the help of Michael, who triumphs over Satan and his tricks, they reach the Savior.

The tone of these plays is far from solemn. They are full of action and tense, taunting dialogue between the ancient enemies, Michael and Satan. The best lines, though, are reserved for the comic banter among the shepherds, who represent "everyman" with all of humanity's foibles and vices. For example, one shepherd declares to his fellows at the beginning of the play, *"Ustedes están siempre viendo visiones. Yo lo único raro que he visto es que a mi bota se le acabó el vino desde antes del mediodía, y no se quién habrá sido."* ("You are always seeing visions. The only strange thing I have seen is that someone emptied my wineskin before noon, and I can't identify the culprit!")

Despite the occasional levity and slapstick that provide comic relief in these plays, they speak of serious matters. On life's journey we must all contend with evil if we are to progress toward God.

Through the *pastorelas* the faith of the people was handed down from one generation to the next—not in a classroom, but through drama and example. These yearly plays were written to be accessible to all: children and adults, the illiterate as well as the more sophisticated. Because of their broad-based appeal they can still serve today as a tool for evangelization.

Parrandas

Parrandas is a Puerto Rican tradition; the word means "party" or "revel." Quite simply, a *parranda* is an announced or impromptu caroling from door to door, which is followed by an offer of hospitality by the head of the household where the caroling is done. In return for refreshments, the visitors may serenade their hosts for hours with their festive music, playing guitars and a mandolin-like instrument called a *cuarto*. Often, a singer will perform an improvised ten-lined, rhymed song called a *controversia* in honor of the Virgin.

A more energetic form of the *parranda* is an *asalto*, literally "assault." Taking the impromptu nature of the *parranda* more literally, the *asalto* group goes to a house in the middle of the night, wakes the host, and then expects to be received graciously with food and drink. It is

a matter of honor for many traditional Puerto Ricans to be prepared during the holiday season to offer hospitality at any time of the day or night.

This Puerto Rican custom bears some resemblance to the Mexican *posadas* since they both highlight the value of hospitality. Guests, especially unexpected ones, may indeed be the Holy Family. Therefore, one needs to be vigilant and prepared to offer all people hospitality when they sing of the Good News!

New Year

While many Latinos have adopted a more secular approach to New Year's Eve, complete with toasts and "Auld lang syne" at midnight, some Hispanic families see the coming of the New Year as a time for prayer and family. It is an opportunity to ask forgiveness for sins, and many people like to celebrate the sacrament of reconciliation on New Year's Eve. Observances may begin with a Holy Hour before the Blessed Sacrament at church earlier in the evening and then continue at home with a festive evening to usher in the New Year. *Año Nuevo* is seen as a passage that is best made accompanied by God and loved ones.

Epiphany: *Los Reyes Magos*

For many Latino groups, the feast of the Magi is the principal time to exchange gifts during the Christmas season. Just as the wise men brought gifts to the Christ Child, so we at this time give gifts to one another in Christ's honor. This atmosphere of generosity and giving can provide an opportunity for the parish to care for those who need assistance. Soliciting gifts of food and clothing for the poor, and arranging a special Epiphany meal for those who cannot provide one for themselves, are all ways that the feast can be grounded in the needs of the community.

The celebration begins with Mass at church. Most families then return to their homes to eat a festive meal, where, as described in the story, a special bread called *Rosca de Reyes* is served. Baked into the bread are small plastic figures of the infant Jesus. The ones who get the infants in their portions will be the hosts or *padrinos* of the celebration marking the end of the Christmas season, the *levantamiento del Niño Dios.*

Candelaria: Levantamiento del Niño Dios

Despite some observations to the contrary, popular religious customs have a certain logic to them precisely because they are intimately connected with life. Just as the *acostamiento del Niño Dios* (putting the Christ Child to bed) is celebrated on Christmas Eve, the season's end is marked by the *levantamiento del Niño Dios* (lifting up of the Christ Child).

Celebrated forty days after Christmas, *Candelaria*, or the feast of the Presentation, celebrates Christ's presentation in the temple in Jerusalem. Brought by Mary and Joseph, Jesus encounters the aged prophets Simeon and Anna. Simeon's blessing and prophecy to Mary end the joyous Christmas season by looking somberly ahead to the passion of Jesus through the eyes of Mary. After hearing the gospel reading for today's feast, few Hispanics would fail to think of the traditional statue of the grieving Mary used during Holy Week. This image, *Nuestra Señora de la Soledad* or *Nuestra Señora de Dolores,* depicts Mary with not one but seven swords piercing her heart. For, as Simeon says to Mary, "This child is destined for the falling and the rising of many in Israel, and to be a sign that will be opposed so that the inner thoughts of many will be revealed—and a sword will pierce your own soul too" (Luke 2:34b–35, NRSV).

The story of Mary and Joseph bringing Jesus to be blessed serves as the backdrop for this final Christmas celebration. Just as family and friends gathered for the blessing of the *nacimiento* in the home after the Mass on Christmas Eve, so they gather on *Candelaria,* when the statue of the infant Jesus is formally "picked up" in order to mark the end of the Christmas season. The custom that links home with church is the traditional blessing of both these statues and the parish's children in the church after Mass. The blessing includes a prayer that the family will be aware of the grace of Christmas throughout the year.

The devotion to the *Santo Niño,* is not restricted to Hispanics. Filipinos, too, have a very lively devotion to the *Niño,* especially during the last week of January. It was the statue of the *Santo Niño,* brought by Ferdinand Magellan (Magallanes) to the Philippines, that is credited with making the first important conversions to Christianity. For Filipinos, then, this devotion is also linked with evangelization and national identity. In parishes where both Hispanics and Filipinos worship, the infant Jesus can serve as a way of bringing these groups together at the end of the Christmas season. The custom of bringing in *Santo Niño* statues for blessing on *Candelaria*—as well as blessing young children during this time—is a common expectation among both Hispanics and Filipinos.

Levantamiento del Niño Dios en la iglesia

Para el levantamiento, los padrinos acuden la casa donde se realizó el acostamiento, donde vestirán al Niño Dios de blanco antes de llevarlo a la iglesia. Se sugiere que antes de irse a Misa de Candelaria (2 de febrero), se rece el rosario de la forma acostumbrada y quienes han participado en él, acompañen a los padrinos a la Misa con la comunidad. Al Niño Dios le pueden llevar en una charola previamente adornada por la familia, de acuerdo a su costumbre local.

Durante el rito de conclusión se invitará a los niños presentes a que pasen al frente y se les bendecirá con una oración tomada del Bendicional, o con la siguiente:

Dios lleno de amor, en Jesús, recién nacido,
bendice a estos niños y niñas,
con la ternura de tu amor.
Acompáñales en sus juegos,
estudios y quehaceres con sus familias;
sé parte de su alegría e inocencia,
a fin de que puedan seguir creciendo en edad,
sabiduría y gracia, al lado de sus padres.
Te lo pedimos en unidad con el Espíritu Santo,
que junto con Jesús
vive y reina contigo, por los siglos de los siglos.
R: Amén.

Lifting Up of the Christ Child at Church

For the celebration of the *levantamiento*—lifting up the Christ Child—the sponsors go to the house where the *acostamiento*—putting the Christ Child to bed—was celebrated and dress the figure in white clothes before taking it to the church. It is suggested that before going to Mass on the feast of the Presentation of the Lord (February 2) the rosary be prayed in the customary manner, then all present accompany the sponsors to Mass with the community. The Christ Child may be carried on a tray decorated for the event according to local custom.

During the concluding rite of the Mass, those children present are invited to come forward for a blessing. Either a prayer from the Book of Blessings *or the following prayer may be used:*

> God full of love,
> through the newborn Jesus
> bless these children with the tenderness of your love;
> accompany them in their games, studies and family chores.
> Be part of their happiness and innocence
> so that they may grow in age, wisdom and grace,
> at their parents' side.
> We ask you this in the unity of the Holy Spirit,
> who together with Jesus
> lives and reigns with you, for ever and ever.
> *R:* Amen.

Para la bendición de las estatuas del Niño Dios antes de la bendición final de la Misa. Puede tomarse una oración del Bendicional, o la siguiente:

> Dios Nuestro, que bendijiste al género humano
> enviando a tu Hijo a la tierra, como revelación
> plena de tu amor por nosotros, tus hijos e hijas,
> te pedimos que bendigas estas estatuas de tu Hijo Jesús,
>   hecho Niño,
> a fin de que nos recuerden siempre tu presencia
> y la necesidad de hacernos como niños,
> para así participar de tu reino.
> Te lo pedimos a ti que eres grande y maravilloso,
> que vives y reinas con tu Hijo Jesucristo,
> en unidad con el Espíritu Santo,
> por los siglos de los siglos.
> *R:* Amén.

For the blessing of the statues of the Christ Child before the final blessing of the Mass, either a prayer from the Book of Blessings *or the following prayer may be used:*

> God our Creator,
> you blessed humanity
> by sending your Son to earth
> as the full revelation of your love for us,
> your sons and daughters.
> We ask you to bless these statues of Jesus your Son,
>   who became a child,
> so that we may always remember your presence
> and our need to become like children
> in order to participate in your reign.
> We ask you this who are great and marvelous,
> who live and reign with your Son Jesus Christ,
> in unity with the Holy Spirit, for ever and ever.
> *R:* Amen.

⚘

Questions for Reflection

1. *Does Christmas end for your family on Christmas Day? Why or why not?*

2. *What post-Christmas traditions have you inherited that you continue to practice today?*

3. *How does the Hispanic celebration of Christmas prepare you for Holy Week? What Holy Week themes do you see in Christmas?*

4. *How does the time after Christmas help you to be more aware of the needs of the marginalized, the poor, the immigrant?*

5. *Christmas celebrates new life. Where do you see new life in your family and parish after the annual celebration of Christmas?*

⚘

1. *En tu experiencia familiar, ¿la Navidad termina el 25 de Diciembre? ¿Por qué si o por qué no?*

2. *¿Qué tradiciones posteriores a la Navidad has mantenido que las continuas hasta hoy en día?*

3. *¿De qué manera la celebración hispana de la Navidad te prepara para la Semana Santa? ¿Qué aspectos de la Semana Santa contemplas durante la celebración de la Navidad?*

4. *¿De qué forma te ayuda el tiempo de Navidad a estar más consciente de las necesidades de los pobres, los marginados y los inmigrantes?*

5. *La Navidad celebra la vida nueva. ¿Dónde percibes la vida nueva en tu familia o parroquia después de la celebración anual de la Navidad?*

Epilogue

I n the Midwest, January winds are rough on the face, making small cuts that crevice the skin. Wind is only one of many hazards for cemetery workers, who stand out in the open in weather that freezes a family's tears almost instantly. The reverence of these workers shows in their slow, rhythmic movements as they lower the coffin into the grave. Moisés is alert to the significance of this moment even after so many years of doing the same thing. It is more than a job for him; it is his small contribution to a family in need. He believes in what he is doing.

This had not always been the case. As he would easily admit, there was a time when he didn't care much about life or death or anything in between. Tempting fate was as easy as waking up in the morning. Dying seemed just as good as living. This all changed one day, but not because anything traumatic happened. There was no miraculous visit from a heavenly messenger. He simply decided that life was worth living, and so he changed. He joined the small community groups of San Martín along with Lupe, his wife. At first, he was quiet, but soon he found himself speaking his mind and even his heart. Tears were not unknown to fall from his weatherbeaten face, yet he felt no shame. Father John was not sure of Moisés at first, but gradually, in coming to know his history, Father John's impression changed.

The January winds continued into February. The warm thoughts of Christmas were now a distant memory as Moisés stood waiting for the funeral hearse to arrive. He remembered the cold, windy night when he and Lupe were walking back home from church after the evaluation of the Christmas meetings and liturgies. Moisés and Lupe decided that the time had come for them to take another step. Words had to become actions. Moisés wanted to do something that he had never done before. Lupe encouraged him by saying that she would help him in any way she could. She had never left him in all the turbulence of the past; she would not leave his side in all the challenges of the present. They would take the lead in preparing Lent and Holy Week. He wanted to know more about this "dying and rising" foreshadowed during Christmas. He was jealous of the way Rutilio and Silvia spoke about it with such conviction. If he had been able to find meaning in the bitter cold wind, he could fathom the depths of this mystery—or at least he and Lupe would try.

Glossary

acostamiento del Niño Dios. Literally, "putting the Christ Child to bed."
The laying of the *Niño Dios* in the crib of the household manger
scene, which takes place after the Christmas Eve Mass.

aguinaldos. Christmas gifts, usually little treats or toys.

altarcito. The home altar, often displaying candles, pictures of deceased
relatives or sacred images.

Año Nuevo. "New Year"; the Hispanic celebration of the New Year is
more religious than in North America and may include the celebration of the sacrament of reconciliation and observance of a
Holy Hour at church before the family festivities at home.

arrullo. The lullaby sung to the *Niño Dios.*

asalto. See *parranda.*

Candelaria, Candelmas. Celebrated on February 2, this day was formerly the feast of the Purification of the Virgin Mary but is now the feast of the Presentation of the Lord. The *levantamiento del Niño Dios* celebrated on this day marks the close of the Hispanic Christmas season.

cena. "Dinner" or "meal"; here referring to the festive meal at home on Christmas Eve.

chronos. A Greek word referring to time that is measured by clocks and calendars, an earthly or worldly time. See also its opposite, *kairos.*

comites Christi. "Companions of Christ"; refers to the three feast days that follow Christmas Day and point toward Lent and Holy Week: Stephen (December 26), John the Evangelist (December 27) and the Holy Innocents (December 28).

compadre, comadre. Refers to a close relationship formed through a sacrament, such as that between godparents and the baptized.

Comunidades Eclesiales de Base. "Small base communities"; small groups formed from households in a neighborhood within a parish. They provide a place for faith-sharing and service.

danza. Indigenous sacred dance that forms part of the liturgical experience of prayer.

Guadalupanas. Members of the parish Guadalupe Society.

intenciones. A Christmas Eve tradition in which each family member offers a petition for the family before the meal.

Los Guloyas. See *Junkanoo.*

Junkanoo. A Christmas tradition among the slaves of the colonial period; it is found today in different forms in Belize and the Dominican Republic and is believed to have begun in the sixteenth and seventeenth centuries, when slaves were allowed to perform their African music and dance only at Christmas.

kairos. A Greek word referring to sacred time, which is transcendent and contemplative, as opposed to standard chronological time, or *chronos.* See also *chronos.*

levantamiento del Niño Dios. Literally, "picking up the Christ Child"; refers to the removal of the Christ Child from the crib on the feast of the Presentation of the Lord, or *Candelaria* (February 2). At home, the Christ Child is taken out of the crib, dressed in new clothes provided by the *padrinos,* and taken to church for a final blessing. Then it is reverently kissed and put away until the next year.

Mañanitas. Mexico's equivalent of the English "Happy Birthday" song. It is always sung to Our Lady of Guadalupe early on the morning of her feast.

matachines. Native American dancers who play a key role in rituals in the southwestern United States. Their *danza* is a form of prayer.

mestizaje. A "mixing," in this case of the Iberian conquerors with the native peoples of America and slaves from Africa, which created the Latino people and culture described in this book.

mestizo, mestiza. A man or woman, respectively, of mixed European and Native American ancestry.

Misa de gallo. Christmas Midnight Mass.

Misas de aguinaldo. Pre-Christmas novena Masses often celebrated before dawn among Puerto Ricans and Venezuelans, among others. See also *Simbang Gabi.*

mística. A term used in this book to describe the Hispanic worldview as conditioned by centuries of contact with the gospel and the clash of three cultural worlds: the European, the Native American and the African.

nacimiento. Christmas crèche or manger scene, often set in an elaborate modern town setting.

Nicán Mopohua. The oldest document that tells the story of the apparitions of Our Lady of Guadalupe to Juan Diego. It was written in Náhuatl, the language of the native peoples, by Don Antonio Valeriano, a Náhuatl scholar of the sixteenth century.

Niño Dios. Christ Child figure (small statue or doll) placed in the parish or household manger scene for the season, often venerated by the faithful with a kiss at the Christmas Eve Mass. Families bring their Christ Child figures to Christmas Eve Mass to be blessed. At home they are central in household devotions—rocked, sung to and placed in the family crib for the duration of the season. On February 2 the *Niño Dios* is taken up from the crib, washed, dressed in new clothes, taken to church for a blessing, and then reverently put away until the next year. See also *acostamiento del Niño Dios* and *levantamiento del Niño Dios.*

Nochebuena. Christmas Eve.

Nuestra Señora de la Soledad or *Nuestra Señora de Dolores.* The image of Our Lady of Sorrows venerated during Holy Week. The image is evoked by Simeon's prediction of the suffering of Christ and Mary (Luke 2:34), recounted on the feast of the Presentation of the Lord, *Candelaria,* the close of the Hispanic Christmas season.

oplatek. The Polish Christmas wafer given out at a family's Christmas Eve meal after being blessed in church.

padrinos. Technically, godparents or sponsors.

panuluyan. Name given to *posadas* in the Philippines.

papel picado. Paper that is decorated with intricate cutouts, used for celebrations.

parrandas. The Puerto Rican custom of house-to-house group caroling in exchange for hospitality, which continues from Christmas to *Los Reyes Magos* (Epiphany, January 6). A more vigorous form of a *parranda* is the *asalto,* in which the revelers may come to a home very late at night demanding food and drink, and expecting to share their music and revelry.

parranderos. Those who perform the *parranda.*

pastorelas. Among Mexicans, allegorical plays that narrate the announcement of Christ's birth to the shepherds and their journey to the Christ Child.

peregrinos. Literally, "pilgrims"; in the context of *posada,* the word often refers to Mary and Joseph.

pésame a la Virgen, el. Condolences to Mary as the sorrowful mother, a popular religious practice during Holy Week in which people express that human, personal relationship toward Christ, Mary and the saints that is the cornerstone of Hispanic popular religion.

pesebres. The Christmas crèche; see also *nacimiento.*

piñatas. Decorative containers of candy and small favors that are hung from the ceiling and broken by blindfolded people with sticks, enacting the human struggle with sin. This Mexican custom for celebrating occurs after each of the pre-Christmas novenas.

pollos. The name for *parrandas* in the Dominican Republic.

ponche. Hot beverage served at home after the Christmas Eve Mass.

posadas. A novena-based devotion that reenacts Mary and Joseph's search for *posada* (lodging) on the night of Christ's birth. The faithful form a procession behind a couple playing the role of the holy pair (or statues representing them). Stopping at a home, they pray the rosary and then sing a song that dramatizes the dialogue between Mary and Joseph and the innkeeper.

"Primero Dios." Literally, "first God"; a common expression among Hispanics meaning "God willing."

rebozos. Women's shawls, often used for rocking or carrying infants.

Reyes Magos, Fiesta de los. Solemnity of the Three Kings (Epiphany), celebrated on January 6.

Rosca de Reyes. A special bread eaten on Epiphany (January 6) that contains little plastic Christ Child figures. Those who find the small infants in their piece of bread will become *padrinos* (sponsors) for the *levantamiento del Niño.* See *padrinos, levantamiento del Niño Dios* and *Reyes Magos, Fiesta de los.*

Santo Niño. "Christ Child." At the end of Christmas Eve Mass, a couple acting as Mary and Joseph may hold the Christ Child figure and the people may be invited to come forward and venerate it with a kiss. See also *Niño Dios.*

Santos Inocentes, Los. The Holy Innocents, whose feast day is December 28; December 28 is also the equivalent of Mexican April Fools' Day, when jokes are played on the unsuspecting.

Simbang Gabi. The novena of Masses celebrated prior to Christmas by Filipinos. See also *Misas de aguinaldo.*

Tepeyac, Mount of. The geographical location designated by Our Lady of Guadalupe as the site of the church she wanted built. This mountain was the sanctuary of Tonantzin, the Aztec mother goddess worshiped by the Aztecs.

villancico. Christmas carol.

Resources

The following resources give a fuller description of the great variety of Latino Christmas customs and provide material that may be helpful in preparing celebrations.

BOOKS

Calvachi Wakefield, Charito. *Navidad Latinoamericana—Latin American Christmas.* Lancaster, Pennsylvania: Latin American Creations Publishing, 1999.

Davis, Kenneth, ed. *Misa, Mesa y Musa: Liturgy in the U.S. Hispanic Church.* Schiller Park, Illinois: World Library Publications, 1997.

Elizondo, Virgilio. *Guadalupe: Mother of the New Creation.* Maryknoll, New York: Orbis Books, 1997; in Spanish, *Guadalupe: Madre de la Nueva Creación.* Buenos Aires, Argentina: Editorial Guadalupe, 1999.

Elizondo, Virgilio, and Timothy Matovina. *Mestizo Worship: A Pastoral Approach to Liturgical Ministry.* Collegeville, Minnesota: The Liturgical Press, 1998.

Elizondo, Virgilio, and Timothy Matovina. *San Fernando Cathedral: Soul of the City.* Maryknoll, New York: Orbis Books, 1998.

Fernández Martín, José Luis. *La Navidad en México: Orígenes y Celebraciones.* 3 volumes. México, Distrito Federal: Publicaciones Paulinas, 1994.

Flor y Canto. Portland, Oregon: Oregon Catholic Press, 1989.

Francis, Mark, and Arturo J. Pérez-Rodríguez. *Primero Dios, Hispanic Liturgical Resource.* Chicago, Illinois: Liturgy Training Publications, 1997.

¡Gracias! Chicago, Illinois: Liturgy Training Publications. (Bilingual journal for Hispanic liturgy).

Pinzón Umaña, Eduardo. *En Nombre de Dios Pedimos Posada, Nueve Noches de Esperanza Antes de Navidad.* Ligouri, Missouri: Ligouri Publications, 1995.

Santiago, Esmeralda, and Joie Davidow, eds. *Las Christmas: Favorite Latino Authors Share Their Holiday Memories.* New York, New York: Alfred A. Knopf, 1998.

Torres, Larry, ed. and trans. *Six Nuevomexicano Folk Dramas for Advent Season.* Albuquerque, New Mexico: University of New Mexico Press, 1999.

Helpful Websites

www.churchforum.org

A Spanish-language church forum offering a comprehensive treatment of Catholicism and religious information from Latin America. From the list of options on this page, choose "Info." At the next page, scroll down to the "Indice Alfabético," where you will find the topics "Adviento" and "Navidad."

www.elboricua.com

Website containing articles from the monthly bilingual cultural publication for Puerto Ricans *El Boricua,* which includes articles about Christmas traditions.

www.mexconnect.com/mex_/feature/xmasindex.html

English-language website containing many articles and images related to Christmas celebrations in Mexico.

www.navidadlatina.com/tradiciones/welcome.asp

Spanish-language site offering detailed listings of Christmas customs for each Latin American country.

webdemexico.com.mx/principal/religion.htm

Spanish-language website from the University of Guadalajara offering in-depth articles on the Virgin of Guadalupe and Christmas customs in Mexico.

Videos

Fiesta! Celebrations at San Fernando. Produced by Thomas Kane. 49 mins. Mahwah, New Jersey: Paulist Press, 1999.

Presents highlights of the liturgical year as celebrated at San Fernando Cathedral.

La Gran Posada: A Christmas Celebration. San Antonio, Texas: Hispanic Telecommunications Network and Family Theater Productions, 1998.

Un Pueblo Sacramental/A Sacramental People: La Boda/Wedding; Pésame/ Mourning the Dead. 30 mins. Chicago: Liturgy Training Publications, 1999.

Presents a wedding and a service of mourning celebrated by different communities with commentary by participants and remarks by the authors of the book *Primero Dios.*

Un Pueblo Sacramental/A Sacramental People: Presentación del Niño/ Presentation of the Child; Quince Años/Quince Años. 30 mins. Chicago: Liturgy Training Publications, 1999.

Presents the presentation of the child and the *quinceañera* (fifteenth birthday) as they are celebrated in different parishes.

Soul of the City/Alma del Pueblo. 28 mins. Houston, Texas: JM Communications, 1996.

Celebrates the liturgical life of the congregation of San Fernando Valley Cathedral in San Antonio, Texas.